KUNG FU

DAVID CHOW AND RICHARD SPANGLER

KUNG FU

History, Philosophy and Technique

U|P UNIQUE PUBLICATIONS

4201 VANOWEN PLACE, BURBANK, CA 91505

ISBN: 0-86568-011-6
Library of Congress No.: 73-14043

DISCLAIMER

  Please note that the publisher of this instructional book is NOT RESPONSIBLE in any manner whatsoever for any injury which may occur by reading and/or following the instructions herein.

  It is essential that before following any of the activities, physical or otherwise, herein described, the reader or readers should first consult his or her physician for advice on whether or not the reader or readers should embark on the physical activity described herein. Since the physical activities described herein may be too sophisticated in nature, *it is essential that a physician be consulted.*

To A-Tse, Tai-Sing, Tai-Chung,
Tai-Lan and Chou Tsu Ping
from David

To Dee, Dutch, Joan and Shane
from Richard

Contents

Introduction

True words are not fine-sounding;
Fine-sounding words are not true.
The good man does not prove by argument;
And he who proves by argument is not good.
True wisdom is different from much learning;
Much learning means little wisdom.
The Sage has no need to hoard;
When his own last scrap has been used up on behalf of others,
Lo, he has more than before!
When his own last scrap has been used up in giving to others,
Lo, his stock is even greater than before!
For Heaven's way is to sharpen without cutting,
And the Sage's way is to act without striving.

—Tao Te Ching, Chapter 81, Arthur Waley translation

When the original ninety-minute pilot film "Kung Fu" hit American television screens in February of 1972, the impact of its popularity shook viewers from their dulled senses of being stuffed by the pap and Pablum servings of normal, hard-to-digest TV fare. After going to a regular weekly series without any great fanfare, millions of viewers made "Kung Fu" the number-one rated show in the United States. It was the phenomenon of the television industry, an action show that emphasized pacifism over violence. Who would have dreamed that a half-Chinese, half-American Buddhist monk with a price on his head and the master of a Chinese fighting art would become the new culture hero of America? Who was this mild-mannered Kwai Chang Caine? What was this strange Chinese fighting art he practiced? How and where did he get his training? Where did his profound philosophical remarks come from? Does the Shaolin Monastery still exist? How do Buddhism and Taoism relate to Kung Fu? What influence has Kung Fu had on other martial arts?

These are just a few of the questions received at the "Kung Fu" technical advisory office at Warner Brothers studios in Burbank, California. Instead of individually answering the hundreds of thousands of letters, we felt an obligation to write, in book form, our interpretation of the evolution and philosophy of this ancient Chinese unarmed fighting system. We make no claims about being encyclopedic in this volume, but we will reveal for the first time in English some of Kung Fu's astounding secrets—the reality behind some of the enigmas. We will unveil the obscure and sometimes weighty history of the Chinese martial arts. Do not let the strange Chinese names or ancient dates put you off from reading further. Certain concrete facts must be conveyed to establish the historical basis of the most refined self-defense techniques in the world.

Most books in English which discuss Chinese martial arts gloss over Chinese names and dynasty dates as being too bewildering or just unnecessary. We disagree. We feel, in reaction to the intense interest, that it is time to be specific, admitting that this is not always possible due to the lack of adequate documented records, particularly during the first, second, and third millenniums before Christ.

From our original sources in China we will describe feats which most Westerners consider impossible. How to walk up the side of a wall. How to walk on sand without leaving footprints. How to incapacitate an enemy with the flick of a finger. The delayed death-producing Red Sand Palm. These will be explained as supernormal abilities available to anyone who wishes to invest the necessary years of training.

While the section on "The Dynamics of Kung" will amaze and possibly shock the reader, the heart of this book is being dedicated to Kung Fu's philosophical essence: "Learn the ways to preserve rather than destroy. Avoid rather than check; check rather than hurt; hurt rather than maim; maim rather than kill; for all life is precious, nor can any be replaced." Kung Fu must be thought of, in its final form and spirit, as an expression of man's indomitable will to survive adversity in the most direct, self-reliant manner possible. This requires only that which nature gave him, a mind and body, rigorously disciplined as an inseparable entity. Within this framework Kung Fu will be presented as an experience which begins on the physical level and gradually deepens to a pervasive philosophy influencing the totality of one's behavior. Of course, techniques producing fatal results will be described, but our stress will be on the art's basic belief in nonviolence: "If there is no contention, there is neither defeat nor victory. The supple willow does not contend against the storm, yet it survives." Or as a Shaolin priest explained a violent act to young Caine in a "Kung Fu" TV episode:

YOUNG CAINE
(understanding)
You are sad, Master, because you took a life.

MASTER PO
Yes . . . to save another.

YOUNG CAINE
(emotionally)
Mine.

MASTER PO
(nods; then)
It may some day become necessary for you to take a life . . . to save an-other . . . or to save many. You will feel as I do, then . . . you will feel sorrow—no matter how evil is the creature you slay.

The first thing that must be established before reading this book is the definition of Kung Fu. Kung Fu is a general term defined as the mastery of an art, an accomplishment or a difficult task through highly concentrated effort. It ultimately means a lot of hard work or practice. Kung—accomplishment, Fu—effort. In Western terms it can be said that Muhammad Ali achieved Kung Fu in boxing; Michelangelo attained Kung Fu in art; Ernest Hemingway reached Kung Fu in literature. This term, induced by Chinese fighting masters displaying their own "Kung Fu," has become known incorrectly in the Occident as the way to express "Chinese martial arts." Although a loose interpretation was made while passing through the language barrier, the English-speaking world of today has accepted the wordage and understands it to mean anything to do with the fighting systems of China. We felt compelled to explain the slip in translation, but instead of launching a terminology crusade, we also shall accept the verbal Americanization of the Chinese martial arts. However, the term was not used regularly until the early Ming dynasty, when novels were flourishing in the fourteenth century. Many of these popular books praised the determined efforts of fighting masters who were ridding a province of invading bandits. "Kung Fu" was used readily to express the successful exploits of the courageous masters. On the other hand, the actual Chinese term for martial arts is Wu Shu, which denotes military arts, training for self-defense and bravery. Wu—militaristic, Shu—techniques. Put into Western historical perspective, the Chinese character for "Wu" appeared in bronze inscriptions approximately three hundred years before the Trojan War (c. 1200 B.C.).

The character that represents Wu Shu is composed of two parts. The first indicates the act of stopping, and the second, is a pictograph of a spear. Together they symbolize the idea of using military power to subdue violent disorder and promote peace by doing away with shields and spears. This was based on the ancient advice that "Weapons are like fire—if not extinguished they are bound to burn the user." This became a credo of the later martial artist who would not resort to using his fighting prowess whenever he wished merely to inflict harm. His art was to be used to serve and protect while avoiding conflict if at all possible. However, should combat be inevitable, the master could render his attacker as defenseless as a water color painting under the relentless pelts of a thundershower.

Today, Wu Shu remains the official term for martial arts in the People's Republic of China, although the emphasis is on its use as a national sport "to serve the people" in the promotion of health. No matter which term is used, Kung Fu or Wu Shu, the relevance of understanding the words in the Western world lies in the demystification of the essence or meaning behind them. This is our purpose. We are participating in the lifting of Kung Fu's centuries-old cloak of secrecy. "To suppress a truth is to give it force beyond endurance." We hope that our modest effort will help to provide an impetus which will further release publicly the beneficial knowledge about the long-enduring martial arts of China.

1.

The Beginnings

Survival of the mightiest was the natural process of life when Paleolithic man prowled the earth in the Stone Age. Venturing from his cave in search of sustenance, the earliest known human was forced to contend with towering and overpowering beasts and reptiles. His physical strength held little chance for outliving the wild creatures. Man's teeth and nails were no match for fangs and claws. Even his legs often were not strong enough to outrun or outjump his animal adversaries. Constantly though he was susceptible to sudden death, self-reliance revealed that he had one superiority over the carnivorous brutes: brain power. The cave dweller used his innate intelligence to create crude weapons to fight his foe at a distance while swinging his arms and legs at vulnerable points against those grappling at close range. At the same time, he continued to watch the techniques of other predators and their prey. Early man, according to anthropologist John E. Pfeiffer in *The Emergence of Man,* advanced the "understanding of his nature by studying the ways of other hunting packs. Furthermore, when he started becoming a big-time carnivore himself, he probably profited from the efforts of his fellow meat eaters by imitating their stalking and hunting methods. . . ." It was either adapt or perish. He found that successful foraging for food was enhanced by group effort and defense against peril was fortified by teamwork. In banding together with his fellow humans he began to establish territorial rights. However, other bands, less fortunate or more aggressive, started to encroach on his hunting grounds. Conflicts arose. Inevitably, man was fighting against man. These haphazard struggles for primitive existence led gradually to the origins of preconceived self-defense techniques. Although precise historical records either never existed or have not been located, scholars generally accept the thesis that the rudiments of martial arts began in different parts of Asia and were perfected in China.

Elements of the Chinese martial arts, now popularly known in the West as Kung Fu, can be traced to the Neolithic Age approximately four thousand years ago. The earliest form of martial arts appears in the story in which the legendary Yellow Emperor, Huang Ti, fought and defeated his enemy, Chi Yuo, by using classical Chinese wrestling methods. This incident occurred in the first half of the third millennium B.C. However, even Chinese historians confess a distinct lack of documented evidence which could prove definitely that the oldest and most sophisticated form of the martial arts evolved from those ancient days of the Yellow Emperor.

Nonetheless, during the Shang dynasty (c. 1523–c. 1027 B.C.) with the first evidence of oracle bone inscriptions and script itself, it again was asserted that wrestling existed. Furthermore, certain fighting movements were developed into a type of folk dance performed by people wearing animal horns on their heads and butting into each other, then grabbing and throwing each other to the ground. This festive demonstration was designed to show strength and virility, as in two powerful bulls contending against one another. In this, the Age of Bronze, archaeological finds have proved that war chariots with horse in harness were common. Spears, arrows, knives and needles were made from bronze, indicating the advancement of fighting and hunting tactics.

Historical records are more plentiful and reliable for the Chou dynasty (c. 1027–256 B.C.), which marked the beginning of the Iron Age. We can ascertain that, as schools of philosophy began to spring up, archery and charioteering (or horsemanship) were two concomitant accomplishments which all gentlemen and scholars were supposed to possess in their efforts to become Chun-tzu, morally and physically superior men. Archery, for example, was included in the curriculum for students between the ages of fifteen and twenty to prepare them for an important ritual called the "Ceremony of Archery." The practice of shooting a bow and arrow had become a refined art that went beyond mere physical training. The skill was considered an integral part of "li," the customary cultural rituals or the sum of all those conventions by which men in a stable society live together in harmony. The classic Book of Odes, a compilation of some three hundred poems circa 700 B.C., celebrates great moments of Chinese ceremony or ritual. Fighting with the fists, Ch'uan p'o, is mentioned in at least one line, "Without the fist, there is no bravery." Therefore, it can be concluded that Ch'uan fa, the way of the fist, already was being practiced by some of the people of Chou, though their specific techniques are not known to us today.

In the second half of the Chou dynasty (770–221 B.C.), from the Spring and Autumn Annals through the Warring States period as iron began to replace bronze in weapons making, it was recorded in the *Records of the Grand Historian,* compiled by Ssu-ma Ch'ien (145–c. 80 B.C.), that there emerged in China a distinctive fighting class that became known throughout the empire. With the decline of feudalism, the ruling house of Chou weakened and subsequently was demolished by constant warfare and disunity. The ambitious feudal lords developed their own separate kingdoms and ruled independently. They persistently sought more recruits to continue the increasingly bitter internecine battles against neighboring states to enlarge or protect their holdings. According to historian Ssu-ma, many poverty-stricken peasants, unemployed artisans and merchants, along with many former warriors, began to respond to the need. Sensing employment and adventure, they became professional men, better known as knights-errant. They roamed from state to state offering their services to beleaguered lords. Most of the knights-errant, according to Ssu-ma, were skilled in military arts with special emphasis placed on swordsmanship. From this piece of information it can be determined that fighting arts were widely practiced by the common people, especially those who were or wished to become knights-errant.

The knights-errant, however, must not be thought of as merely mindless mercenaries; they had their own respected chivalric codes. They served not only royalty but ordinary citizens in distress. It was said that "a knight [shih] dies for one who appreciates him." In their courageous, Robin Hood-like concern for justice, they would offer their swords in defense of those wronged while "risking death for others without a thought for their own safety." "They always meant what they said," Ssu-ma relates, "always accomplished their intended mission and always honored their promises." Dr. James J. Y. Liu wrote in *The Chinese Knight-Errant* that "historically, knight-errantry is a manifestation of the spirit of revolt and nonconformity

in traditional Chinese society, sometimes lying underground and sometimes erupting to the surface. Its ideals are admirable, though these have
not always been realized in practice, and may have even provided excuses
for lawlessness. It is further possible that the ideals of knight-errantry inspired the moral codes of secret societies of a subversive kind." What is
probable, however, is that the moralistic principles of the knights-errant,
coupled with their chivalrous devotion to visionary ideals, made a powerful
impact on succeeding martial arts masters who became convinced that
their power should be used only for self-defense and rescuing the helpless.
Thus, during the rebellious turmoil of the Chou dynasty, even as Lao Tzu
and Confucius were being born, some fundamentals of systematized martial arts were devised for the first time in China.

As the groundwork was being laid slowly for future martial artists to
build upon, the foundation for the future of China was being formed rapidly in the third century B.C. The impetuous and superstitious revolutionary leader Huang Ti became China's first unifier (221–210 B.C.) by
remarkably welding together the vastly disjointed regions into one political
unit known as the Ch'in dynasty. Adhering to military strategist Sun Tzu's
theory of the absolute power of the prince, "The First Emperor" was determined to consolidate his conquests with a strong hand. In efforts to protect
easily accessible frontiers against warlike neighbors, Huang Ti, using
forced labor, constructed extensive sections of what later came to be called
"The Great Wall of China." When finally completed during the Ming dynasty (A.D. 1368–1644), The Great Wall was the longest fortified barrier
in history (at about 1,400 miles in length over mountains, valleys and
rivers), and a brick, earth and stone monument to the toil and suffering of
hundreds of thousands of workers.

Acting on the advice of Li Ssu, his cold and calculating legalist minister
of state, the Emperor brought down upon himself the everlasting oppro-
brium of subsequent generations of Chinese. He attempted to subjugate his
people by a kind of early "thought control" or "brainwashing." All books
which conceivably might have contained even a germ of an idea antagonistic to his rule were ordered to be burned. These included official state
chronicles, the Classic of Poetry (Chih Ching), the Classic of History
(Shu Ching) and philosophical works. Most of the books, considered
scarce before this "edict of fire," were hand inscribed on bulky slips of
bamboo and wooden tablets. However, not all was lost in the literary holo-
caust. Exempted from the proscription were treatises on such necessities as
medicine and farming, official imperial chronicles to glorify Ch'in and its

power, and tracts on the foretelling of future events by supernatural means. (Fortunately, many of the condemned books were resurrected later from memory and hidden copies.)

The Emperor had been obsessed with finding the means to achieve immortality. With popular Taoist magical practices failing to provide the proper elixir, he died during the search. Huang Ti wanted not only to manipulate the minds of his subjects but to dominate their bodies as well. He prohibited the practice of martial arts, resulting from his fears that the masses might somehow rise and destroy his empire. The people were not permitted to carry weapons of any kind. As an ensuring precaution, all fighting instruments not required by Ch'in troops were seized and melted down. Death was the routine penalty for those who failed to obey the Emperor's decrees. Although it is believed that some members of the Ch'in dynasty continued to practice martial arts in secret until 206 B.C., three years after Huang Ti's death, when a massive internal upheaval occurred, ending in the overthrow of the Ch'in heritage. (Not entirely, however, for "Ch'in" seems to live on even today as the basis for our word "China.")

After the swirling dust of disorder settled, a brutal but prudent former outlaw, Liu Pang, assumed the throne of the Han dynasty. He said arrogantly that he had won the empire on the back of a horse, emphasizing strength over moralistic philosophy. However, he later amended his contention by saying that he advocated the Confucian belief that government must be for the benefit of the governed. Confucius said that benefits could be produced through royal example. The Emperor, who became known as Kao Tsu during his seven-year reign (202–195 B.C.), said that he agreed while adding his strong force to the gentlemanly Confucian example.

As a man of the people, Emperor Kao sanctioned the end of serfdom and permitted the resumption of martial arts practice throughout the realm. According to the *Han Shu,* the four-hundred-year dynastic history authored by Pan Ku, military arts became a vital part of governmental policy. Army training was accentuated. Swordsmanship and hand-to-hand fighting methods were incorporated into the regular military preparation programs. A talented soldier could gain high rank and great stature by being proficient with the sword. This was particularly evident during the zenith of the "Celestial Empire" under Wu Ti, the "Military Emperor," who, at the age of sixteen, began his reign in 140 B.C. as the fifth Han regent. This brilliant tactician ruled for the next fifty-three years, expanding and protecting his empire with his heralded military campaigns. For his exceptional deeds Wu Ti demanded superbly trained men to become his generals: "A bolting or a kicking horse may eventually become a most valuable animal. A man who is the object of the world's detestation may live to accomplish great things. As with the intractable horse, so with the infatuated man; it is simply a question of training."

Meanwhile, the common people were adapting martial art forms for their own physical training. In the later Han dynasty (A.D. 25–220), about the time that Buddhism was introduced to China in the first century, a commoner, Kuao Yee, created a new style of fist fighting called Chang-shou, meaning "long arm." Although the exact techniques have been lost, since the oral teachings were never recorded, it is suspected that Chang-shou had some influences on the development of the martial arts.

During the following Era of the Three Kingdoms (A.D. 220–65) a celebrated physician, Hua-t'o, was said to have developed the use of anesthetics in treating painful afflictions. Known for his legendary cures, the good doctor became one of the first advocates of preventive medicine. Hua-t'o wanted to avoid or curtail illness through his series of exercises which he called "Five Animals Play." The physical movements, designed to strengthen the body, were created from his observations of the tiger, deer, bear, ape and bird. He maintained that "simple exercises would evoke perspiration to cleanse the body." In turn, Hua-t'o said, "The body would become lighter which would trigger a healthy appetite resulting in the consumption of invigorating nourishment." These basic exercises obviously were not practiced to enhance fighting prowess, but they can be considered to be preliminary initiators of later forms of Kung Fu based on animal movements. However, there is no doubt that martial arts, in various stages of limited refinement, already had existed in China for at least two thousand years. The difficulty of proof lies in the fact that no known martial arts schools were established before the Era of the Six Dynasties (A.D. 264–581). While there were no organized schools of martial arts in existence before the sixth century, outside of imperial troop training, nevertheless, some fighting practices were known to the people through obscure masters who deigned to instruct a few selected disciples.

2.

The Father
of Shaolin Ch'uan

Despite the legends and tradition still speaking for much of the vague early history of Chinese martial arts, it can be asserted with fair certainty that unarmed defense principles were advanced through Ch'an Buddhist religious practices during the sixth century. The holy man considered by most modern sources to be the father of the martial arts is Bodhidharma, the formidable and enigmatic twenty-eighth Indian patriarch exalted by orthodox Ch'an tradition. Bodhidharma (called P'u-t'i-ta-mo by the Chinese) lived circa A.D. 448–527. It is said that this venerable abbot, who was the third son of a Brahman king, left his monastery in Southern India to spread the Ch'an Buddhist faith to China.[1] Unverified chronicles[2] relate

[1] Ch'an was the Chinese transliteration of the Sanskrit word "dhyana," signifying yogic concentration, which has come to be better known in the modern West by its Japanese interpretation, Zen.

[2] The standard Ch'an version was "The Record of the Transmission of the Lamp," compiled in A.D. 1004 by Tao-yuan of the Northern Sung dynasty. There was Ch'i-sung, also of the Northern Sung (A.D. 960–1126), author of *An Essay on the Orthodox Transmission of the Dharma*. Another was a Ch'an historical document, *Ch'uan Fa-pao Chi,* found at the turn of the twentieth century in a sealed cave at Tun-huang in Northwestern China. It was said to be compiled by Tu Fei (Fang-ming) between A.D. 700–10 (T'ang period). An earlier record was *Biographies of the High Priests,* by Tao-hsuan, written in A.D. 645 during the early T'ang dynasty. The earliest source appears to be the *Lo-yang Chia-lan-chi,* authored by Yang Hsuan-chih in A.D. 547. But do not expect your neighborhood library to have these ancient texts. They are extremely rare.

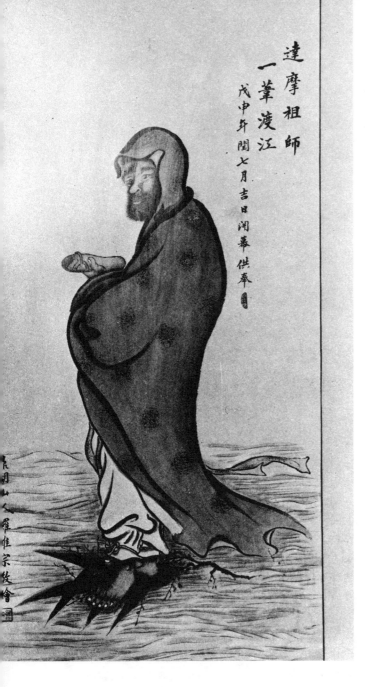

達摩祖師
一葦渡江
戊申年閏七月吉日閉幕供奉

A reverential Shaolin artist's rendering of Bodhidharma, believed to be the father of Shaolin Temple boxing. This painting depicts the great master making a fruitful journey across the Yangtze River while riding on the blades of a reed.

that in his missionary zeal he walked hundreds of miles to reach Northern China, not only surviving the perilous journey along the trails fraught with bandits, but managing to cross the treacherous and freezing Himalayan Mountains. His initial destination was Nanking, where he was summoned before the court of Liang Wu Ti (A.D. 502–49), monarch of one of the kingdoms established during the Six Dynasties period.

Emperor Wu, anxious for the sage to bless his own self-proclaimed devout contributions to Buddhism, asked Bodhidharma, "We have constructed many temples, copied the holy scriptures, and supported many monks and nuns. What merit is there in our conduct, Reverend Sir?"

"No merit at all," he replied. "Those are inferior deeds containing vestiges of worldliness which are akin to shadows in the forest. They only appear to exist. In reality they have no substance. The only true work of merit is Wisdom, pure, perfect and mysterious, which is not to be won through material acts."

Appalled at the response, which to him indicated that his presumed great efforts were being condemned, the Chinese ruler inquired again, "What, then, is the holy truth in its highest sense?"

"In vast emptiness there is nothing holy," said Bodhidharma. Finally, in exasperation, the Emperor asked, "Who is it, then, confronting me now?"

"I know not, your majesty," was his baffling answer. Dumfounded, Emperor Wu dismissed Bodhidharma and stalked off in an uncomprehending rage as the mystical wise man with the great black beard walked serenely out of the royal palace never to return. The Emperor, feeling that he could buy his way into Buddhahood, simply was not aware of the true essence of Ch'an, which is the perception of self-nature. He did not realize that what he had asked was not verbally answerable from the Ch'an viewpoint— "The nature of the mind when understood, no human speech can compass or disclose. Enlightenment is naught to be attained, and he that gains it does not say what he knows." Salvation could only be achieved by inward enlightenment, i.e., illumination could not be outwardly communicated. Material offerings were considered secondary, if not totally in vain. If he had understood this, he would have reached at least one level of realization. As Ch'an monks say, "Understanding—this one word is the source of all mysteries."

As an ancient legend contends, "Riding on the blade of a reed (a leaf-shaped ferryboat), Bodhidharma crossed the Yangtze River and went north to Loyang," the capital of Honan Province, where, in the neighboring densely forested, mountainous countryside, he found the Shaolin Ssu (Young Forest Temple) along the northern side of Shao-Shih Mountain south of Sung San Mountain. The monastery, built by Emperor Hsiao Wen of the Northern Wei dynasty (A.D. 386–534), had become famous as the site for scholarly translations of immense works of Buddhist scripture into Chinese. Monks purportedly toiled as scribes in shifts, day and night, translating over six hundred sacred Sanskrit books into their native language. Upon Bodhidharma's arrival, however, the Fang Chang ("Head Monk") feared that the sage's reformist Ch'anism, which dismissed book learning as irrelevant, might disrupt the monastery's more traditional tenets of Buddhism. The Fang Chang directed him to remain outside of the temple. Thus, this last Indian patriarch, who was to become China's first Ch'an patriarch, took refuge in a nearby cave. Bodhidharma "originally came to China to transmit the teaching and save deluded beings." His task was seemingly impossible. Dana R. Fraser, in *The Recorded Sayings of Layman P'ang,* said that "though teachers of various types of Buddhist **meditation had preceded him, none had been able to establish a school or line of disciples." Nevertheless, he was determined to show that Su**preme Wisdom had nothing to do with orthodox performances, ritualistic practices, or rendering Sanskrit to Chinese. Western culture finds his solution difficult to fathom, if not completely incredible. This monumental mystic began to sit in cross-legged meditation facing a rock cliff next to the Shaolin Monastery. He remained there in absolute silence for nine years. This "Ch'an sitting" was thought to aid those who encountered insurmountable obstructions. But do not get the impression that Bodhidharma was staring at the rock wall for twenty-four hours a day. This, despite some fanciful Ch'an histories, is not true.

One account suggests that he meditated on a mat of leaves for two-hour periods at dawn and dusk with further contemplation inside his cave. The wall-gazing Brahman, as he subsequently was termed, was said to be able to hear the screeching of the ants crawling along the venations of the rock face. Gradually, monks, scholars and peasants began to visit this spiritual eccentric, although it was always a one-way conversation, since he remained rapt in meditation, refusing to speak to anyone. They left as they came, unenlightened, unable to discern the meaning behind his philosophy of silence. This was the Great Master's missed point, for his was "a silent transmission of the seal of the mind." Bodhidharma was saying, "Put an end to the formation of all external relationships and be rid of any vehement desires inside your heart; then with a mind like a wall, indifferent to outside disruption, you may enter into the truth."

Once, during meditation, sleep overcame him. This so offended his profound sense of discipline that when he awoke, according to a most certainly apocryphal description, he cut off his eyelids to forever thwart sleep. Tea shrubs sprang up in the same spot where he had cast away the eyelids. The tea leaves later helped monks stay awake. (The contradiction in this legend appears to be the fact that tea drinking was not introduced until the T'ang dynasty, A.D. 618–907, long after Bodhidharma's death.)

In less inspired Ch'an biographies, it is related that at the end of the nine years Bodhidharma's large, deep blue piercing eyes did exactly that; his powerfully steady gaze had drilled a gaping hole in the cliff wall. After seeing the eye-riveted orifice, the stunned Shaolin Fang Chang could no longer resist his obviously superior authority. Bodhidharma entered the Shaolin Monastery gates to become the first Tsu (patriarch or, literally, ancestor) of the Ch'an sect in China.

"The incomparable doctrine of True Buddhism can be understood only after long, hard discipline and by enduring what is most difficult to endure, and by practicing what is most difficult to practice. Men of inferior virtue and wisdom will not comprehend it. All their labors will come to nothing," he told his first disciple, Hui-k'o.

Imagine this strict disciplinarian's grim disapproval when he saw his monks constantly drowsy or slumbering during the vital meditation exercises. He realized that their flaccid and emaciated bodies could not stand the test of prolonged mental austerity. Although Buddhism is aimed specifically at the salvation of the soul, Bodhidharma explained to the monks that body and soul are inseparable. This unity must be invigorated for enlightenment. The legend continues that physical fitness became a part of Shaolin life with his introduction of systematized exercises to strengthen the body and mind. Not only was health perfected, but self-defense movements were devised later from Bodhidharma's knowledge of Indian fighting systems. These early calisthenics (in-place exercises only) marked the beginning of Shaolin Temple boxing. Bodhidharma transmitted orally his exercise forms which were transcribed by later monks as (1) *The Muscle Change Classic* or *The Change of Sinews,* (2) *The Marrow Washing* and (3) *The Eighteen Hand Movements of the Enlightened One* (The Eighteen Lo Han Shou).

Strictly speaking, the Great Master's exercise regimen does not appear specifically designed for boxing, since his main purpose was to physically inspire his monks to greater spiritual heights. The forms, however, do indicate an awareness of boxing techniques, possibly more, as Dr. Kenneth Ch'en suggests in *Buddhism in China,* that Bodhidharma "taught the monks a style of boxing for self-defense as well as for reinvigorating the body after a period of meditation. In this manner arose the Shaolin style of boxing which became famous in later Chinese history." Wen-shan Huang's translation of Bodhidharma's "Treasures," as they are known in the Orient, shows a standing exercise beginning in a "riding horse step" posture, that is, with legs spread apart and slightly bent while the back and head are held straight up; the body weight is distributed evenly on both feet, which are parallel to each other: "Hold clenched fists tightly upward at waist level, elbows close to sides. With utmost firmness, thrust the left clenched fist diagonally to the front, turning the fist over so it faces down when fully extended. Return to preparatory position. Repeat the exercise on the right side, alternating five times on each side." This exercise, with slight variations, continues to be practiced in basic Kung Fu training and seemingly will remain as the basis for many striking techniques in the future.

However, Bodhidharma's primary concern was the cultivation of Ch'i (intrinsic energy), the acquisition of control over this internal force and using its power to mold superior monks. Ch'i, derived from ether or matter, is the vital body element which can be energized by the regulation of breathing to produce stamina and endurance along with the feeling of well-being and mental balance. "Breath is the flywheel of life," as Chinese cultural historian Huang interprets Bodhidharma's legacy. Every exercise was based on respiration; for example, in a natural standing position, hands against the thighs, "Raise the two arms slowly to the chest, breathing in. Push hands forward, with a stretching movement, until the arms are extended, wrists bent, palms pointing forward and fingers upward, breathing out. While maintaining the stretch, move the hands fully to the left and right with the palms turning upward. At the same time breathe in and try to visualize the Ch'i, or vital energy, arriving at the tips of the fingers." This emphasis on Ch'i should be considered to be Bodhidharma's main contribution to the art of empty hand fighting. For without this basic and essential energy source, Kung Fu development would have remained as hollow as an automaton, employing mere physical motions, lacking mental mastery.

Bodhidharma's story continues as legendary history with at least one pious biographer asserting that poison was mixed with his food and drink on several occasions by his rivals, but he did not succumb because he was immune to earthly harm. Finally, however, it is written that the Great Master did ingest a poison (some say by his own hand) and die at the reputedly self-revealed age of one hundred fifty years, this lengthy age according to biographer Tao-hsuan.[3]

On the day of his death, as Ch'an historian Tu Fei would have us believe, Sung Yun, a lay official of the Northern Wei dynasty, was returning to China from a Buddhist literary expedition when he encountered Bodhidharma on the trail. He noticed that the Great Master was wearing only one sandal. The sage told him he was crossing the desert to the Pamirs and then to India. Sung Yun later told Bodhidharma's disciples of the brief meeting. When they opened his gilded and lacquered cloth coffin, the astonished adherents saw that his remains were gone. All they found was one sandal. This was one Ch'an version of the mystic's passing. Still others reported that since the faith was flowering in China—"one flower opens five petals, and the fruit ripens of itself," according to a Bodhidharma verse—it was time to travel to Japan, where the Ch'an founder planted his Buddhist seed and vanished.[4] No Western scholar takes much of this tradition very seriously, but a multitude of Chinese Ch'an devotees believed a considerable portion of it; many still do and continue to herald Bodhidharma as the originator of Kung Fu.

Although it is known that some forms of boxing did exist in China prior to the arrival of Bodhidharma, specific records about how systematized they were remain to be unearthed by scholars. However, the essence of the Great Sage's incipient martial arts heritage was absorbed, enriched and refined by succeeding Ch'an masters to become the powerful yet graceful Shaolin Temple boxing, sometimes called Shaolin Ch'uan (Shaolin Fist) or Shaolin Ch'uan Fa (Way of the Shaolin Fist). Shaolin Ch'uan began to become well known. Word of its benefits spread to members of another famous Chinese faith, Taoism, which taught avoidance of force through contemplation and reason. Taoist priests became increasingly attracted to the Shaolin system because of its peaceful and nonoffensive philosophical foundation.

[3] The authors suggest that it might be more realistic, in light of other alleged facts, to say that Bodhidharma died at seventy-nine.
[4] Buddhism is known to have reached Japan about A.D. 550, which would seem to indicate that Bodhidharma had been dead for nearly twenty-five years.

3.

Taoist Contribution to Kung Fu

From the tumultuous uprooting and the dead-white ashes of warfare of the Spring and Autumn Period followed by the Warring States Era, there blossomed some of the brightest and liveliest schools of philosophy known to mankind. "Death and disorder abound," the Book of Odes explains. "The talk of the people is bad since no one assuages their grief." They sought wisdom for the correct conduct of human affairs and a moral cure for the evils of society. This longing for philosophy led emperors to personally patronize learned scholars and profoundly thoughtful advisers. Their reasoned guidelines were preserved on bamboo parchment. These inscriptions may have been the first oriental flourishes of the pen attempting to overpower the finely honed sword of devastation.

The greatest of all Chinese philosophers to arise out of the centuries of revolutionary instability and excessive treachery was the imposing figure of Confucius (K'ung Fu-tzu, c. 551–479 B.C.). In the intellectually deep wake of Confucianism, more philosophical concepts were formulated through what came to be known as the "Hundred Schools of Thought." (The Chinese "Hundred" may be defined as "many" in Western terms.) The most influential, after the Confucians, were the Taoists, who directed their teachings toward the individual search for a higher form of physical and mental existence. Since Taoism (pronounced Dowism), despite its matter-of-fact practical aspects, has been called "the most enigmatic of all Chinese philosophies," it might be helpful to compare it with the more recognized and better understood Confucianism. Beauson Tseng, a contemporary Chinese philosopher, has summed up the main difference in these terms: "If the Ways of Heaven of Nature (the Tao) be likened to an ocean, the fellow who exerts himself and makes wise use of his knowledge of hydrodynamics to swim in a beeline to his chosen destination—is a Confucianist. The other fellow, who holds that the most ideal spot for him is where the winds and currents will of themselves carry him to—is a Taoist. The more man lets science have free play, the more science can be made to serve man. Tao behaves much in the same way as science." While most of the other philosophical schools, including the Confucians and Legalists, were promulgated for sociopolitical problem-solving through regulations and laws, the anarchistic Taoists advocated that "The more restrictions and prohibitions there are in the law books, the more thieves and bandits there will be."

Troubled Taoist thinkers felt it best to transcend earthly suffering by withdrawing from the ill-conceived man-made "civilization" and join or rejoin the natural forces of life. They were convinced that this could be accomplished by living absolutely detached from organized society as contemplative hermits deeply secluded in the wilderness of the mountains and forests. Unlike Buddhist tenets, Taoism does not promise emancipating nirvana or entry to the Pure Land of Bliss at the end of spiritual pursuit. Neither does it offer salvation that delivers men from misery after death. On the contrary, the Taoists treasure life because to them living is supremely sweet and enjoyable after being secured by nature's rhythms.

The approximate literal translation of the "Tao" is the "Way" or "Path," although, according to the Taoist classic literary work *Tao Te Ching* (pronounced Dow Duh Jing), its meaning is inexpressible in words, "The Tao that can be named is not the everlasting Tao." The eighty-one "flowers" (beautiful chapters) of the *Tao Te Ching* (meaning "The Way and Its Power") are attributed to Lao Tzu, the traditional father of Taoism in the fourth century B.C. Ssu-ma Ch'ien contends in his monumental work of history that the mysterious sage was a native of Lu I County in Honan Province. He lived approximately a hundred years (c.? 580–480 B.C.). "Since he had the appearance of an old man in his youth, Lao Tzu ('Old Master') became his sobriquet. His true name was Li Erh. He served ably in the Chou court as the guardian of the imperial library. However, he began to lament over the constant corruption surrounding him. Confronted with abysmal living conditions, compounded by the decline of Chou, Lao

Tzu decided to leave his native land and pursue virtue in a more congenial atmosphere. As he was about to pass through the final mountain pass, the gatekeeper, Yin Hsi, recognized him as a renowned philosopher and asked him, 'Oh, Master, before you retreat from the world, would you kindly write down your way of living for me?' Lao Tzu consented and wrote his *Tao Te Ching,* his entire philosophy compressed into some five thousand pithy ideographs. The great mystic then left the Middle Kingdom (China) and traveled to the west on a water buffalo. He was never seen again."[1]

Whether this tale is accurate or whether this profound little book was compiled by Taoist thinkers over the span of some centuries is not essentially a problem. Authorship is not that important. It is the philosophical content that matters. What is relevant is the fact that the aphoristic *Tao Te Ching* has exerted a tremendous influence not only in China but the rest of the world. It continues to do so. There are over forty versions of it in English with at least seven hundred commentaries in Chinese. However, in strict fairness it must be said that certain Taoist ideas were considered long before the appearance of Lao Tzu. If we examine the *I Ching* (Ee Jing), known as the *Book of Changes* in English, we will discover many Taoist concepts. In this classic book of divination, dating perhaps as far back as the sixteenth century before Christ, we see the first mention of Tao and Yin and Yang, dealing with the duality of nature: "Yin and Yang, together they are called Tao." Therefore, we may safely deduce that Lao Tzu did not originate his entire philosophy. He absorbed what he felt to be the best thoughts of his country's intellectual heritage, distilled them, added to them and founded the first organized school of Taoism.

In its early phases there was no worship of supernatural deities. To the philosophical Taoist, the ontological elements of all universal beings and even the universe itself are combined into Tao. They existed before the universe was born. Tao has no limits. Its existence is eternal. Tao is not a supernatural force. It is the ultimate principle of the universe. Tao is the prime element from which everything is created in nature. If this sounds puzzling and abstract in the Western sense, it must be understood that from the Chinese scientific standpoint Tao stands on solid ground with its explanation of the mysterious existence of the universe. Tao is composed of two forces represented by Yin and Yang. Yin is characterized as the negative force of darkness, coldness and emptiness. Yang stands for the positive energy which produces light, warmth and fullness. These alter-

[1] We have translated this quotation directly from Ssu-ma Ch'ien's biography of Lao Tzu in *Records of the Grand Historian,* which some scholars treat as the official biography of the Taoist sage. But it must be said that many modern historians assert that Lao Tzu is at best a mythical figure or if he did actually exist there are no proper records to prove it conclusively.

The famous Chinese Yin-Yang symbol surrounded by eight trigrams which figuratively express nature and its changes. The Yin-Yang symbol, also called the "Double Fish" diagram, represents two opposites residing together. In the heart of Yin will always be found a small part of Yang, and vice versa. Within strength is found weakness; within hardness, softness; inactivity, activity. Inside a sleeping newborn babe there rests a strongly beating heart.

nating forces are indestructible and inexhaustible. They contradict as well as complement each other. This "eternal duality" may be explained further as the primordial paired potencies that regulate the universe.

> *"The myriad of things carry Yin and embrace Yang."*
> —Tao Te Ching, *Chapter 42*

"Te," or "the Power," is the manifestation of Tao in substantiality or corporeity, the most important element in any existence, created by the interaction of Yin and Yang. This means that every object or substance possesses positive and negative elements within itself. Therefore, we can understand the opposing forces of life: Birth begets death, rise includes fall, day expects night, hardness opposes softness, male-female, resist-yield, hot-cold, wet-dry, motion-stillness, push-pull, coarse-smooth, contraction-expansion; that which condenses will disperse; that which disperses will condense. Herein lies a major East-West difference in philosophical attitudes. The Westerner, à la Shakespeare's *Hamlet,* would say, "To be or not to be? That is the question." The Taoist sage, on the other hand, would say, "To be and not to be. That is the answer!" Yin-Yang opposites unite. This is the Taoist law of nature. To really be vitally alive, to truly feel life's offerings, is to know the highs and lows, the exhilaration of the mountaintop and the descent to the valley, and to accept and enjoy not one but both. Life's highs are most invigorating; there is also fertileness to be found in the lowest valley. The phenomena of materiality originated from the antithetical forces of Yin and Yang. Any effort aimed at altering this natural law would be futile.

The followers of Taoism, along with the Chinese people in general, felt that the cosmos was composed of five elements or forces: water, wood, fire, metal and earth. Each element produces or changes another in cyclical succession, as metal cuts wood, water extinguishes fire, wood penetrates earth, fire dissolves metal and earth halts water; or water creates wood, which turns to fire, which fertilizes earth, which responds by producing metal followed by water. Matter and energy are indestructible. They can change their forms but can never be destroyed.

The elements move in continuous cycles responding naturally to one another. When one force becomes strong, the second becomes weak. This process continues ad infinitum. The universe may be thought of as a vast circle encompassing increasingly smaller circles wherein there is no beginning and no end. Natural events take a path of spontaneous creativity through regular alternations of phenomena (e.g., sunrise-sunset) that proceed unobtrusively without effort.

Lao Tzu postulated the idea of Wu Wei, usually translated as "nonaction," to explain man's appropriate relationship with nature. On the surface Wu Wei means "not to do anything" or "to remain totally inactive." To the pragmatic Occidental mind this might seem to be a ridiculous concept of inconsequential idleness, but with concentration the deeper meaning will be realized. Nonaction does not mean idleness, apathy or indifference to the Taoist; it rather implies the unresisting attitude that he adopts as he abides and communes with nature.

> *"The Tao never acts, yet nothing is left undone."*
> —Tao Te Ching, *Chapter 81*

To be suitably "not active," man must also discard ambitious desires, for desire is the initiating force which engages man's active movement. Since the greatest revelation of Tao lies in "stillness," that "stillness" must be preserved in the inner being by dismissing all motives that would disturb it or draw it into action. Do not move in response to outward inducements but only to that which is within and spontaneous. When man eventually transcends his self-ego and merges himself with nature, he is then in union with the Tao. Thus, Lao Tzu emphasized that man should be aware of the active principle but should stay with the passive principle.

> *"Know the masculine (active principle), but keep*
> *the feminine (passive principle)."*
> —Tao Te Ching, *Chapter 28*

This is not to say that the Taoist resigns himself to that of weak and timid docility. There is rather the strong attitude of unflinching fortitude in the Taoist disposition of patiently receiving or enduring without resistance. He has learned to be tenacious in his hopes. He knows that eventually the sun will shine brightly from behind the darkest of clouds. This is the essence of "achievement without doing."

The passive principle of Wu Wei connotes spontaneous responsiveness to nature. Deliberate efforts to alter nature can only lead man into confusion and entanglement. This typical Taoist concept of spontaneity undoubtedly inspired much of the philosophy behind the physical training of Kung Fu. Kung Fu was not an art developed to perpetrate violence. It was designed to be responsive to outside or hostile forces only when necessary, i.e., when the serenity of nature was violated. However, many styles of Kung Fu have incorporated "deliberate efforts" in attempts to achieve mastery of what may be called external or "hard" muscular systems of self-defense. In basic training, a Kung Fu devotee would have to go through a series of strenuous exercises with "deliberate efforts" to ensure proper body conditioning. Following continuous physical practice, day after day, year after year, his highly controlled punches, kicks and blocks would become mentally refined to the point of spontaneous reaction. Any oncoming danger could be thwarted by an intuitive or "natural" response with his carefully developed protective visceral reflex, an inseparable part of his being. His previous motions with planning would become instinctual motions without planning. An antagonist's thrusting fist to his head could be avoided with the instinctive ease of batting away a fly from the nose. Amplifying on this sometimes difficult to comprehend but vital martial arts concept of spontaneous aptitude, we suggest that any motion may be formed to be "Wu Wei" by dedicated practice. In simple terms, a professional typist may be considered a Wu Wei master at a typewriter. The eye reads the letter "A"; the finger automatically, without deliberate thought, hits the "A" key. A highly proficient typist is able to strike one hundred twenty words a minute. From the self-defense point of view, a highly proficient Kung Fu master, using his arms, legs and head, conceivably could hit efficiently a dozen opponents in a no-holds-barred street mob attack at least one hundred twenty times within sixty seconds, although this would never be required, since only a few naturally responsive blows (as a result of proper training) would be sufficient to deter a single assailant. In many instances merely one well-delivered Wu Wei punch will have the effectiveness to incapacitate an attacker. It is thus possible that the twelve-man mob, should none of them run away, could be rendered defenseless in twelve seconds or less with a master's automatic and efficacious movements in neutralizing one obstacle after another.

Despite having the capability of crushing an assailant's body, a true Chinese master, steeped in Taoist philosophy, would never dishonor his art by reducing himself to such base, senseless aggression. He would say, "To rejoice in the conquest is to rejoice in murder." Kung Fu should be used only to preserve the natural flow of life, to avoid, divert, neutralize or blend with any destructive force. This art of self-discipline must not be used to seek out and subdue or control others. This fundamental attitude of Kung Fu is based on a major Taoist precept, as Lao Tzu philosophized:

> *"Those who actively initiate will be defeated;*
> *Those who hold fast to anything will lose it.*
> *Therefore, the Sage is never defeated because he is passive,*
> *and never loses because he is detached."*
> —Tao Te Ching, *Chapter 64*

The highly influential Chuang Tzu, Lao Tzu's most heralded successor and the greatest Taoist writer whose existence has been definitely authenticated (365–290 B.C.), wrote that Wu Wei meant a totally unassumed, unstrained doing. It is the perfect action of doing nothing which is forced or unnatural. Those who follow this calm course will actually accomplish more. Conscious effort can only disrupt the spontaneous accomplishment of the universe moving in continuous harmony. Chuang Tzu's poem "The Need to Win" strikes the bull's-eye on this point:

> When an archer is shooting for nothing
> He has all his skill.
> If he shoots for a brass buckle
> He is already nervous.
> If he shoots for a prize of gold
> He goes blind
> Or sees two targets—
> He is out of his mind!
>
> His skill has not changed.
> But the prize divides him.
> He cares.
> He thinks more of winning
> Than of shooting—
> And the need to win
> Drains him of power.
>> *The Way of Chuang Tzu,* XIX, 4
>> Thomas Merton translation

通微顯化張真人像

Taoist priest Chang San-feng, the
legendary creator of T'ai Chi
Ch'uan, "The Grand Ultimate Fist."

From the physical standpoint Taoism's most important contribution to
the Chinese martial arts has been the creation of T'ai Chi Ch'uan, a complete balance and muscular control system initially designed to maintain
health, calm the mind, and increase longevity. Self-defense methods were
devised later for highly advanced stages of training. They became so effective that T'ai Chi Ch'uan was recognized as one of the superior schools of

traditional Chinese "boxing." The essence of T'ai Chi Ch'uan is based on the Taoist conception of T'ai Chi, which may be characterized as the "Grand Ultimate." T'ai Chi, written about first in the ancient *I Ching,* represents the primary cause of the existence of the universe.

Some have contended that Tao represents the origin of the universe. This is incorrect. Although Tao is said to be the universal principle that constitutes the material world, it possesses a motion of the positive and negative force revolving within itself. It cannot generate itself. It is, instead, generated from T'ai Chi. Tao, as the necessary element of the universe, comes from the vast, static and serene state of nothingness known as T'ai Chi. It is soft, passive and tranquil, yet it continues to be the generator of the most powerful and active element in our earthly system. T'ai Chi, as the reality of the universe, is the abode of Tao, the ultimate law of the universe. There is no supernatural power attached to the "Grand Ultimate," nor is there any force in T'ai Chi itself. It signifies a "dynamic tranquillity" residing in a state of nothingness.

In presenting Taoism's outstanding features relating to Kung Fu, we must emphasize that no force exists within the tranquil state of the "Grand Ultimate." Thus, T'ai Chi is said to possess a soft quality. From this quality Yin and Yang are generated within the context of Tao. The "myriad of things" in the universe are produced from the resulting interaction of Yin and Yang. According to this theory of T'ai Chi, the supreme universal ultimate is softness. "The hard and powerful will disintegrate; the soft and yielding will prevail." This essential Taoist belief may be compared with the Christian religious proclamation that "The meek shall inherit the earth." The same thought is there, merely approached from another path. The Taoist path, it must be said, always seemed to lead to water, a favorite life-supporting image. This mysterious and elusive substance symbolized the Way and its power. Water was emblematic of the unassertive, the inconspicuous, and the imperfect always seeking home "in the low ground," which was the "dwelling place of Tao."[2] As we interpret Lao Tzu's thought: "There is nothing under heaven more soft and yielding than water. Yet nothing can equal water's strength. Hard and resistant things

[2] Since perfection would constantly attract imperfection or a diminution of that state of being, the Taoist unresistingly accepted the lower level of imperfection. "To be perfect is to invite deficiency; to rise is to invite a fall." This is why cripples and hunchbacks play a significant part in Taoist literature. Being considered as "incomplete and imperfect," they perhaps can become more mentally attuned to the "natural order" of the universe than those who are purportedly more physically complete. "Be twisted and one shall be whole," said Lao Tzu. "Be crooked and one shall be straight." He meant that true wholeness and straightness may be attained only by returning to the Way.

can find no way of damaging it. The weak overcome the strong; the gentle overcome the violent. Everyone under heaven realizes this, yet no one utilizes this knowledge."

However, one shadowy figure in Taoist history did attempt to put this beneficial knowledge into practice. An obscure Taoist priest, Chang San-feng, is believed to have been the creator of the satisfying exercise system and gentle martial art of T'ai Chi Ch'uan, "The Grand Ultimate Fist." Although the dates of his birth and death are unknown, various historians have placed Chang in the Sung, Yuan, and Ming dynasties. If we can rely on the recorded *Dynastic History of Ming,* as compiled by Ch'ing scholars, this eccentric mystic was tall and robust with a heavy beard (an indication of vitality in China). Unconcerned about his physical appearance, Chang was said to have constantly worn the same quilted coat and straw hat regardless of the weather conditions. For Chang had but one Taoist thought on his mind: "My own destiny depends upon myself and not upon heaven." This meant that Taoism represented an individualistic philosophy of salvation; therefore, Chang's primary pursuit was to find out how to preserve his life and avoid harm and death. He left his native province of Liao Tung in Northern China, gave up a prominent magistrate's position, and began a peripatetic search for methods of immortalization. During his itinerant quest for physical perfection he spent ten years at the Shaolin Monastery mastering Ch'an Buddhist meditation and self-defense arts. Despite becoming a revered Shaolin Ch'uan master, Chang felt that his personal goal remained unfulfilled. He decided to retreat to the verdant Wu Tang mountain range in Hupeh Province. Noted for its twenty-seven picturesque peaks, the Wu Tang Mountains had always been a favorite hermitage of the reclusive Taoists. As the legend tells us, Chang was contemplating inside his hut when, around high noon one day, he heard some strange noises outside. Peering out at the commotion, Chang saw a snake coiled for action, his head raised, hissing in defiance at a predatory hawk perched in the pine tree above. The strong bird swooped down in expectations of catching an easy dinner. While trying to pin down the snake with its viselike gripping talons, the bird began a vigorous pecking attack, but the reptile repeatedly evaded the onslaught by circular twisting and winding away from the direct thrusts of the hawk's sharply hooked bill. The snake attempted to secure the bird's neck with its slithering tail. The hawk raised its right wing to parry the attack. Then the snake coiled partially around the bird's left leg. The hawk roughly shook the leg and violently fluttered its wings to disengage the limbless creature. Fiercely stabbing again and again, the hawk tried to poke and pierce the snake's head. The reptile, in its constant wavy and spiral movements, never offered a vital target to the powerful beak or curved talons. As the bird became fatigued from its continuous but fruitless attacks, its movements became momentarily unbalanced. In that second before the hawk was going to fly away, the snake struck back with a whip-like elongation of its coiled form. So accurate was its venomous aim that the unprepared bird fell dead almost instantly. After observing this life-and-death struggle, Chang realized that he had witnessed a perfect example of a yielding force overpowering a superior strength. He recalled the ancient adage: "What is more yielding than water? Yet it returns to wear down the rock." Supported by his knowledge of the Shaolin martial arts, Chang commenced to study and organize the actions of the snake and bird, along with the movements of clouds, water and trees swaying in the wind. From this inspiration the classic T'ai Chi Ch'uan system of exercise was formed. Calling upon the Yin-Yang principle where opposites interact with each other as a means to an end, Chang based his system on the elongation, expansion or full stretching out of muscles before they were contracted, constricted or pulled in. He sought perfect muscle control, with one movement blending into the next. T'ai Chi Ch'uan may be considered as the first physical therapy program specifically conceived to promote a sound body for longer life.

Self-defense cannot be considered at this point because Chang had made it quite clear that, in his determination to find the secrets of immortality, T'ai Chi Ch'uan was not created for the purpose of fighting. It was aimed at preserving and prolonging life. This is not to imply that by practicing the "Grand Ultimate Fist" exercise system one can physically live forever, but it was designed to supplement the pursuit of longevity. The amassing of Ch'i was also thought to be an integral life-enhancing force evoked through breath control. Thus, proper breathing forms were incorporated into T'ai Chi Ch'uan. In efforts to accumulate an abundance of Ch'i the Taoist would usually practice two additional techniques: imbibing certain pharmaceutical concoctions to preserve the body, i.e., through elixir by way of alchemy, and nourishing Ch'i through mental cultivation. Eliminating the first method as sometimes dangerous and for the most part an "unnatural" development devised by some subsequently divergent Taoist "religious" cultists, we feel that the latter practice of meditation and regulation of the respiratory system is most important, especially in the polluted environment of the twentieth century. The Taoist believed that, through his own supremely concentrated breath control, he could inhale the Ch'i of the universe into his body and fuse it with his own self-energized Ch'i. This combination could only result in a healthful extension of life.[3] This practice demands extraordinary patience and consistently deep meditation. The practitioner, after clearing his mind of extraneous thoughts in a kind of "fast of the mind," must focus only on the constant feeling and sound of the inhalation and exhalation of his respiration. This experience will enable one, in time, to circulate and direct the power of Ch'i into any part of the body.

The proper cultivation of Ch'i has always been difficult to explain in words, but Chinese commentators have continually made their interpretations over the centuries. One respected viewpoint is found in the writings of historian-philosopher Ch'en Yuan-teh, who analyzes Ch'i to mean Pang Jun, or "original vital essence." Ch'en makes the point in his *History of Ancient Chinese Philosophy* that at the moment of birth the body is composed entirely of Pang Jun. If this "original vital essence" can be preserved inside the body, then life can be "immortalized." By "immortalized" Ch'en infers a prolongation of life rather than absolute physical immortality, although certain devout Taoist mystics would disagree and say that eternal life on earth can be accomplished through their strict regimen.

Ch'en continues his Taoist thesis of life-preserving possibilities by saying that the "original vital essence" must remain intact or be saved from decay by keeping the body as "supple as a babe's." The difficulty, according to Ch'en, "lies in protecting the 'original vital essence' from evaporation." The farther man gets away from his primal state, the closer he is to the extinction of death.[4]

---

[3] Obviously, the ancient Taoists, in their idyllic hideaways permeated with continuously fresh air, did not have to contend with the smog and other pollutants that currently plague virtually every modern city in the world.

[4] Do not presume that since the Taoist constantly sought a longer life that he feared death. He fully and fearlessly accepted death, recognizing in the Yin-Yang of Tao that with life there is death. He merely tried to slow the ever-advancing tide of the Yin (Death) force while cultivating the elongation of the Yang (Life) force. Death was born calmly as a natural part of the cyclical continuum. Not fearing death, neither did he feel pain. H. G. Creel interprets this point in *A History of Philosophical Systems:* "The Taoist reasoned, being absorbed in the Tao he could not be hurt because he recognized no hurt; one who cannot be hurt is impregnable; and one who is impregnable is more powerful than all of those who would hurt him. Thus the Taoist sage is the chief and the most powerful of all creatures, imbued with the majestic power of the Tao, the universe, itself." However, this mystical reasoning later proved to be the undoing of many a Chinese martial artist during the Boxer Rebellion of 1900. Convinced of their own physical invulnerability, they charged headlong into oncoming lead bullets. Many "Boxers" were sent to an unexpectedly early rendezvous with the death level of the natural cyclical order on earth. They misread or forgot one of the essences of the philosophy in their xenophobic fanaticism—all Taoist books excoriate martial vainglory and military exploits as totally wasteful meddling. The *I Ching* sums it up thus: "Needless violence and self-glorification upon completion of a difficult undertaking cause the man to fall back into misfortune."

When man is born he is soft and weak;
When man dies he becomes stiff and hard.
Thus, the stiff and unyielding follow death;
The soft and yielding follow life.
                    Tao Te Ching, *Chapter 10*

Most people tend to stress an active life, which, in the process, depletes Ch'i as the vital life-force. The Taoist would contend that life is shortened with the diffusion of Ch'i. It is forever lost. It cannot be recovered. Therefore, one must do all he can to sustain and hold that "original vital essence" within the body. This went as far as preserving the life-giving fluid of the sex act. (Seminal emission was avoided by the Taoist with understanding women aiding him to cause his semen, with a mixture of the woman's vital juices, to revert into his body and flow back into the brain, creating what might be called a body charge.)

Ch'en comments that all of the Taoist methods of immortality are designed to preserve the "original vital essence" of Ch'i in order "to maintain the original natural goodness of man." As in the "enlightenment" of a Ch'an Buddhist, the Taoist acquired Ch'i through "feeling" rather than through "talking." On the other hand, the Taoist, to a large extent, acquired it through motion while the Buddhist settled for seated meditation. The Taoist concluded that sitting meditation might induce numbness or a lack of circulation in the body. T'ai Chi Ch'uan was thus created, as a supplement to traditional internal cultivation, to be a standing meditation with slow, concentrated movements. Taoist sages maintained that "Meditation in activity is ten thousand times superior to meditation in repose."

To the Westerner, meditation has meant dwelling in contemplation in a sitting or certainly static position. However, to the Taoist meditation has more far-reaching implications. Meditation is not necessarily motionless. When a person commits his entire mind and body to a certain performance, no matter whether he is concentrating on sweeping a floor or walking along a beach absorbed in the enjoyment of the sunset, he is said to be in meditation. Hence, T'ai Chi Ch'uan may be considered to be the "ultimate" moving meditation, a meditation in motion. It is the Taoist external effort to assist in the enhancement of the internal cultivation of Ch'i. In a writing attributed to Chang San-feng, on *Cultivation of the T'ai Chi System,* he said:

T'ai Chi Ch'uan encompasses a totality of effort. Meditation, the first step, is the soft and tranquil effort of internal cultivation. The movements of T'ai Chi Ch'uan are the active, external part of the cultivation. One must combine external and internal, activeness and passiveness, hardness and softness, in order to achieve the ultimate goal.

T'ai Chi Ch'uan is sometimes described as "poetry in motion." The art contains movements which are so varied that they put into play every part of the body with harmonious design and graceful patterns. Each form carries a poetic name such as: "Wave Hands like Cloud," "Carry Tiger to Mountain," "Fair Lady Works at Her Loom," "Golden Cock Stands on One Leg," and "Partition of Wild Horse's Mane." The smooth ballet-like elegance of T'ai Chi Ch'uan, with its feeling for beauty, does not readily reveal the fact that beneath the slowly flowing external forms of loveliness there rests one of the fastest, most effective fighting systems in the world. The original T'ai Chi Ch'uan is composed of 108 basic movements executed with a continuous stream of aesthetic deliberateness and clarity, balance and awareness. Each motion has a functional meaning far beyond the basic tranquillity produced by the exercise.

The body becomes so light and agile that, according to the classic *T'ai Chi Ch'uan Ching,* awareness will be so heightened that the additional weight of a feather will be felt as a brick placed on the chest. "The body will be so supple and sensitive that a fly will not be able to land on it without causing an instant reaction."

Chang San-feng is supposed to have said that the true self-defensive power of T'ai Chi Ch'uan "is rooted in the feet. It develops into the legs, is directed by the waist, and functions through the fingers." Faced with unavoidable combat, the T'ai Chi Ch'uan practitioner remains completely relaxed in mind and body. Herein lies the uniqueness of T'ai Chi Ch'uan. Many fighting systems depend on hard muscular movements which create tension and tightness; restrict movement and speed. An attacker may have massive power at his disposal, but a T'ai Chi master will never receive that force. He will maneuver the antagonist into a position where the brute force will be neutralized or used against the opponent himself. This maneuvering is always accomplished with circular movements which harmonize the flow of Ch'i, whereas linear, straight line responses tend to stifle or break the stream of Ch'i. "Always round off your corners, don't ever have any sharp edges," as T'ai Chi Master Daniel Lee says. "T'ai Chi flows like a freeway or expressway, uncongested with no body turnoffs or detours. The arm may be compared to a turned on garden hose. If it is sharply bent or constricted, the flow of the water ceases. It is the same with the arm. If it is tightly bent or pinched, the flow of Ch'i will be reduced to a mere trickle." Add to this the fact that a T'ai Chi adept will constantly keep his circle moving with mercurial fluidity; his opponent will never be presented with an easy stationary target.

The master knows that a weak spot, an Achilles' heel, will always exist even in the most powerful of men, and most assuredly that vulnerability will be found near the heart of strength. Obviously, if an attacker throws an extended left punch at his head, a clear opening is offered momentarily to the chest, ample time for the master to react with a kick literally to the heart. This is part of the grand design of T'ai Chi Ch'uan: Forget the predominant Western demand for someone to "overpower" an antagonist; dismiss any personal desires or emotions in the midst of conflict; instead, follow the enemy's intent by permitting him to "overpower" himself. By assisting him to extend his manifested desire a little more, his own exertion will subdue him. Should the reader retain only one thought from this chapter, let it be to seek the Yin within the aggressor's Yang. Find the weakness within his strength. After instantly analyzing his attacking style, his weakness will reveal itself. His stronger Yang force may then be dissipated by the master's Yin force absorbing power strikes within a circular pattern. The unstoppable direct force will never hit the immovable object in T'ai Chi because the master will be moving and the force will be stoppable. The perfect weaving of the dynamics of motion, coupled with slow and deep breathing under the absolute control of the mind, enables a T'ai Chi master's body to express a litheness and buoyancy wherein great strength is not needed for great power. Most of the power comes from the attacker and is redirected against him with tranquil movement.

The principle of always seeking tranquillity within movement means to withdraw from an enemy's attack. To know when to retreat and where to stop is to avoid a collision of forces. The wise adept, therefore, discards excessive, extravagant or extreme movements. He confines his motions to just what is necessary for defense and no more. He will not overcommit himself by lunging or swinging recklessly. Instead, he will bide his time, keep his block up, and counterattack only when the opponent has overreached himself to the point of imbalance. Then, using an arm "soft as cotton on the outside, hard as a steel rod on the inside," he will grasp the onrushing aggressor and propel him in the same direction in which he was already moving. That increased momentum usually causes the adversary to lose control and fall.

This concept is often expressed by masters comparing the mind-body unity with a tall, shrubby bamboo never breaking in a violent storm. The treelike bamboo always stoically yields to the howling and pushing wind. It flows naturally with the wind's direction, bending with it. However, the moment that the storm withdraws or lets up its fury the bamboo may spring back with tremendous whiplike power of its own. As with the bamboo, the body must bend and yield in the face of violent attack. Only in this way will the body avoid being broken or seriously hurt. Any blow received, no matter how forceful, will have the effect of slamming into a feather cushion. The impact is received without injurious shock as the soft flexible bag may be returned to its desired shape; in the master's case, by spontaneously rebounding against the opponent to quell his aggression. This is part of the mastery of resilient gestures or recoiling responses which invariably surprise the supposedly stronger attacker. As an example, study the form known as "Snake Creeps Down" (She Shen Hsia Shih). If an opponent suddenly attacks you by throwing a right cross at your head, as your head avoids the punch grab his right wrist with your left hand and pull it downward, using his thrusting momentum. Should he then begin to lift it up, parry his hand upward with your left forearm. At the same time, strike his groin with your right fist (or palm). The same form includes another reaction should an attacker punch at your chest with his right hand; press it downward with your left hand as your body recoils away from his thrust. If he strikes at your right temple with his left hand, press it down with your right hand while slipping your head away from his blow. When both his hands are neutralized, the opponent may attempt to kick you in the crotch with his right foot. Lower your body, which helps to withdraw the target from the oncoming kick. Receive the foot in your grasping hands. Hold the heel firmly, raising it a little with your left hand, while your right hand pushes the middle part of the sole of his foot (or shoe). Then throw it forward with both hands as you simply and rapidly lift up your body. The antagonist should end up on his back, if not his head.

T'ai Chi Ch'uan, as the active part of a dynamic tranquillity, represents the most important contribution of Taoism to Kung Fu. Taoism, as a total philosophy of living, represents a vital part of the Chinese cultural heritage and, in general, is a prime source of Chinese mental attitudes. T'ai Chi Ch'uan may be regarded as the acted-out part of this philosophy. This may be the main reason why the art still prevails and is being practiced as a combination exercise and self-defense system by untold millions of Chinese. Occidentals are just beginning to reap some of the benefits of this ancient art, which has become the most popular physical-mental discipline in the world today.

The practice of "Chinese shadow boxing," yet another term for T'ai Chi Ch'uan, can be of benefit to anyone at any time during the day, although Chinese exponents contend that the only time for this elaborate ritual is the first thing in the morning, and the earlier the better. This means that at five or six o'clock every morning in city parks, on building rooftops or in country gardens, millions of Chinese enthusiastically perform their T'ai Chi Ch'uan exercises with intense, almost trancelike concentration to exclude everyday concerns from their minds. It is thought best to face the east dur-

A professor of Chinese culture and master of T'ai Chi Ch'uan, Daniel Lee, of Los Angeles, performs a full attack move with "Golden Rooster Standing on One Leg." This features a groin kick and right palm to the face. However, Professor Lee does not emphasize the offensive element, saying that T'ai Chi Ch'uan appears to be the "newest 'in thing' in the West's continuing search to find peace and tranquillity."

ing practice to better receive and absorb the energizing radiance of the sun as it rises. The adepts, young and old alike, discover that these slow motion calisthenics invigorate each day and consistently promote better health. Older practitioners seem to benefit most from the practice. The renowned Chinese writer-physician Han Su Yin (famous in the West for her best-selling novel *Love Is a Many-Splendored Thing*) says that "just to see these old people move lithely about, keeping their joints free from arthritis and rheumatism, is really an indicator that this regular exercise is good. It has an enormous value, especially for people over forty, in guaranteeing that they will not suffer from these painfully crippling diseases. Having practiced T'ai Chi Ch'uan myself, I would recommend it wholeheartedly. It's made me feel excellent; it provides relaxation from mental strain, but, scientifically speaking, T'ai Chi Ch'uan should not be considered as a miraculous cure-all for all ills." Today the vast majority who practice T'ai Chi Ch'uan do so mainly for the improvement of all round well-being, specializing in the development of breathing and the stimulation of blood cir-

An exercise stance of Nei Kung designed to absorb the power of the air. Eighty-five-year-old Kuo Ling Ying, originally from interior China, resides in San Francisco, where he is known as America's greatest master of Nei Kung. As he expresses his martial arts philosophy: "Big moves are not as polished as short moves. Short moves are not as polished as stillness."

culation, rather than for its great value in subduing an assailant. However, advanced students naturally acquire "Nei Kung," an enhanced power of sensory perception, as they progress to the higher levels of the "Grand Ultimate Fist." "Nei Kung" is an "inner strength and sensitivity" based on the principle of Ch'i, meaning that all energy in the body may be concentrated at one focal point.

The master, in a sense, becomes a "sun" of energy. He radiates a constant over-all strength which is minuscule compared to his totally focused power. As a magnifying glass, he may absorb and concentrate the widespread healthy radiance of his "sun" into one selected pinpoint of fiery magnification. His natural "heat" will always, through great training with a great sifu (master), become intensified by hostile stimuli resulting in magnification toward the offending point, even though it be unseen, unfelt or unheard. That acquired inner "heat" of awareness, the goal of every martial artist, is truly a supreme protector. This internal energy, according to T'ai Chi masters (and most other martial art masters), either gives warning of an impending blow before it reaches its intended mark on the body or enables the would-be victim to withstand the punch without injury or pain.

Legendary stories have been told claiming that antagonists have broken their knuckles while striking a master's cheekbone. The master would walk away unharmed. This may sound mystical and most likely illogical to the Westerner, but to the T'ai Chi Ch'uan master it becomes a natural benefit of the art. He who is one with the Tao is "beyond all harm" and enjoys "tranquillity in the midst of strife."

While T'ai Chi Ch'uan represents the first and foremost style of the "internal" martial arts, there are two other, more recently revealed systems which are richly embellished with principles of what came to be known as the Wu Tang school of the "Grand Ultimate Fist." T'ai Chi's most noted and more strenuous descendants are Pa Kua Ch'uan and Hsing I Ch'uan. Pa Kua Ch'uan evolved through obscure Taoist origins emerging in the nineteenth century as a highly effective "soft" system of Chinese boxing. Pa Kua literally means "eight trigrams." One of the early fabled emperors of China, Fu Hsi (2953–2838 B.C.), has been credited through legend with inventing the eight symbolic trigrams after pondering the scarred markings on the back of a tortoise shell. The trigrams later were incorporated into the *I Ching,* the classic book devoted to interpreting the significance of the symbols. The Pa Kua are usually depicted in a circular diagram composed of eight trigrams. Each trigram consists of three broken or unbroken lines. The continuous line denotes the Yang, or male element; the divided line marks the Yin, or female complement. The eight trigrams, figuratively expressing the evolution of nature and its cyclical changes, represent heaven, earth, metal, wood, water, fire, soil and man. Each trigram has a specifically designated position within the diagram, although each possesses a distinctive quality by itself. By squaring the eight trilinear kua, sixty-four different circumstances may be produced which cover the full circle of the ever-changing human condition. These *I Ching* conditions became naturally realized self-defense expressions of Pa Kua Ch'uan. The how to live and let live movements of propitious action reflect perfectly the all-encompassing range of the hexagrams.

Pa Kua Ch'uan, by emphasizing circular evasion and palm attack, epitomizes the *I Ching* adage that "Man may remove all obstacles through quiet perseverance. Unseen power can move heavy loads." The Pa Kua adept attains mastery of this art through a series of eight postures. These postures are based on an ingenious inspiration of applying various animal forms to the eight trigrams. The main motions are named for and demonstrate the key revolving and rotating actions of the dragon, tiger, horse, ox, elephant, lion, bear and ape. Each of these animals possesses a quality similar to the particular trigram with which it is identified. Just as all of life's expressions are found in the interactions of the eight trigrams, Pa Kua sifu assert that literally all possible body movements are found within the gradations of these postures. These are practiced in what is called "walking the circle," the principal exercise leading to the perfection of Pa Kua Ch'uan. Internal power, the primary essence of "walking the circle," is never developed through fierce or intense practice with tight muscles.

Again, as in T'ai Chi Ch'uan, naturalness is the key word. Tense movements do not exist in properly executed Pa Kua Ch'uan: Flow easily; a powerful feeling and awareness will result.

The unusual aspect of this "martial art" is that it does not contain specific "fighting" techniques as most other styles do. There are no emphatically directed methods of kicking or fist striking. Instead, Pa Kua Ch'uan is a marvelous system of defense created to avoid intended aggression through the elusive beauty of unseen movement. The master may perform baffling circular gyrations causing him to vanish before the opponent's eyes. Whereas he actually has circled behind his attacker for a fraction of a second, sufficient time to incapacitate him with an open (or closed) palm blow. Featuring focused internal strength, the palm strike will provide more than enough power to discourage the antagonist. This is all that the Pa Kua Ch'uan practitioner needs—circular avoidance movements followed by palm strikes. All basic, to the point, but quick and effective. Pa Kua Ch'uan, although confining itself to a brief regimen of forms, demands absolute perfection of the exercises. If these are mastered, the disciple may adapt his body to move away from conflict situations, then respond with sharp palm strikes. Kicks are not considered to be necessary, but, if needed, low foot strikes are used. Attempts to penetrate the circle of a Pa Kua Ch'uan master would be folly for a street fighter, especially one used to head-on linear punching and kicking. Thus, this "Eight Diagram Fist" discipline, covering the circular spectrum, definitely has something to offer the student who wishes to master defensive body motion supported by the least amount of violent aggression.

The creator of Hsing I cannot be authenticated with any historical accuracy, but it seems that the short forms of this compact and flowing style became known publicly in China during the seventh century with tradition maintaining that a General Yueh Fei originated the system in the Sung dynasty. Hsing I, often learned in conjunction with Pa Kua Ch'uan, is definitely considered to be the most martial of the three leading internal systems. Its more aggressive and direct nature of hair-trigger responses is evident in the five main forms which relate to the universal elements: **1)**

Pounding/Fire, 2) Crushing/Wood, 3) Drilling/Earth, 4) Splitting/Metal, and 5) Crossing/Water. Hsing I, meaning "Form-Will," implies the harmonization of mind and body by unifying the five element forms with proper deep breathing. The mind "wills," the body obeys. Chuang Tzu said that "There is no deadlier weapon than the Will! The sharpest sword is not equal to it." Each of the basic exercises benefits certain vital organs— Pounding stimulates the heart, circulation and small intestine; Crushing, the liver and gall bladder; Drilling, the spleen and stomach; Splitting, the lungs and large intestine; and Crossing, the kidneys and bladder. This is why Hsing I is also called a "healthy way of life." In pursuing a unity of thought and action, oblique movements are emphasized. A Hsing I stylist will never counter aggression with straight ahead motions. He will usually move by instantaneously sidestepping away from a strike, trapping the offensive thrust, and countering with a linear blow of his own. Forty-five-degree shifting avoidance movements are common. As in the other internal styles, Hsing I aims at throwing off the antagonist's center of gravity and redirecting it to subdue him. As Hsing I masters like to put it, "An acorn properly placed on a railroad track may derail the train." Closed fist punches are used, as are kicks. However, kicking techniques are normally confined to strikes below the waist because the Hsing I stylist is taught that a big motion is a wasted motion. Each basic form, like nature's elements, has the ability to promote or destroy each other. Just as it takes water to nourish a tree, a fire may burn the tree to the ground. However, one tablespoon of water is unable to douse a raging forest blaze. Should a Hsing I student have a superior fire form with his attacker only able to summon a weak water form, the water will not put out the fire.

Therefore, all of the five basics must be mastered through dedicated repetition for eventual efficient performance. In addition to the five mandatory forms, variations on the movements of living and mythical beings are incorporated into advanced Hsing I training. They are usually combined, according to the school, with selected motions of the tiger, ape, horse, alligator, fighting cock, chicken, swallow, ostrich, eagle, bear, snake, iguana, dragon and phoenix (t'ai bird).

Hsing I and Pa Kua remain relatively unknown, if not absolutely unknown, in the West. It appears that these two systems, more esoteric and not as flashy as many other forms of Kung Fu, will remain obscure at least for the present. Traditionally, Pa Kua and Hsing I masters have been extremely circumspect about revealing their arts, especially for commercial reasons. While there are a few schools teaching these styles in the United

States, the legitimate sifu will not actively seek out students in a businesslike manner, as certain other oriental martial artists have been prone to do. Hsing I and Pa Kua have no relation to money-making, rather stressing "inner" values and a concern for morality itself. It is hoped that Westerners will seek out these arts for themselves, as many are now pursuing the benefits of the better known T'ai Chi Ch'uan. Westerners must understand that a true master will never knock on people's doors or advertise on radio and television in attempts to sign them up for classes. This just is not done by Hsing I and Pa Kua masters. In paraphrasing a Taoist thought of Chuang Tzu, "The master seeks no advantage, makes no plans, engages in no business. With my boys I only seek Tao."

Taoism, with its emphasis on man's oneness with nature and contentment, has inspired the greatest internal or "soft" systems of all the Kung Fu arts. Taoist thought, physically expressed through T'ai Chi, Pa Kua and Hsing I Ch'uan, has imbued the Chinese people with much of their poise, serenity and patience which have made it possible for their magnificent culture to endure. Taoist philosophy, an essential ingredient of the total Chinese spirit, made such a powerful impact on Kung Fu over the centuries that Taoism has become, indeed, an integral and inseparable part of the Chinese martial arts:

> The Way is a void,
> Used but never filled:
> An abyss it is,
> like an ancestor
> from which all things come.
>
> It blunts sharpness,
> resolves tangles;
> It tempers light,
> Subdues turmoil.
>
> A deep pool it is,
> Never to run dry!
> Whose offspring it may be
> I do not know:
> It is like a preface to God.
>
> —*Tao Te Ching*, Chapter 4
>   Raymond B. Blakney translation

4.

External Styles of Kung Fu

The Chinese martial arts encompass the full spectrum of systematized physical actions ranging from the unrelenting hardness of a steel pile driver to the caressing softness of a rose petal. As in the rosebush, Kung Fu inherently contains protective thorns to discourage disruption and to ensure the sweetness of life. While thorns remain static in their perpetual defense of roses, the human body should be kept supple and flexible, constantly prepared to react to danger from any angle in efforts to preserve life. This would indicate that there is an enormous combination of protective responses from which to choose and master. And, indeed, there are. As different fighting styles developed over the centuries in China, many techniques were devised. Weapons were invented to meet special needs of certain dynasties. Even military strategy was designed to suit the times. But wherever the arts evolved, in military or temple training, they flourished with many Chinese masters adding their own favorite nuances of movement. In addition, different families originated, adapted and revised literally hundreds of styles from all over China. Fathers passed their knowledge discreetly, mostly in secret, to selected members of their clan. Due to the distinct personalities of their descendants, plus environmental and societal differences, the inherited systems were often changed to suit the particular ideas, attitudes or requirements of the times.

Today some martial arts historians claim that there are approximately 360 Chinese self-preservation systems. This figure might sound like a wild exaggeration, but it could very well be fairly accurate. It would even be a conservative estimate when it is realized that Kung Fu really has meant so many different things to so many hundreds of masters during the past three thousand years.

All of these styles combined undoubtedly hold every possible defensive and offensive movement somewhere within their systems, which were named not only for their characteristic techniques, but for animals, mountains, rivers, provinces, families, heroes, religious figures and even insects.

Some disciples were known to have changed their grand master's teachings with a variation of a few steps or fifteen degrees in a turn, or by using a closed fist rather than an open palm. These changes lead to a number of "new schools." By carrying on with some or most of the techniques of his grand master, the "new" master, with only minor variations of his own, would place his name on the "new school" banner to satisfy his own hidden ego or desire for recognition.

On the other hand, new systems emerged naturally when various masters left their native provinces during times of turmoil to settle in more peaceful areas. This often happened, for example, when northern masters moved south, changing their styles to blend with the land and people.

Furthermore, there has always been the tendency for martial artists not being able to agree on all aspects of their systems. This is often the case even when individuals supposedly belong to the same school. This is understandable if we can accept the fact that not all men are physically equal. Some people have stronger arms, some have stronger legs. Some men can run faster, some can jump higher. Others move faster while others hit harder. So when the question is asked, and it constantly is, "Which style of Kung Fu is the best?" it is impossible to answer because there is no "best" system of Kung Fu. They all have their special merits, although, since they are all part of a "system," they contain potential flaws or restrictions. Just as men cannot be considered to be perfect, prescribed or organized fighting systems should not be thought of as infallible. With different physical potential, one style may be well suited for one student but extremely difficult for another. Should long and high kicks be a special feature, obviously, a tall and long-legged student would tend to have an advantage over a fellow student who might be quite short with stumpy legs.

In American terms, a coach would never send in a five-footer to guard against the aggressive scoring moves of a Kareem Abdul-Jabbar, who at seven feet three inches would easily dominate the action. By the same token, a small, even tiny person has the greatest chance for success in a personal duel of horse racing. A big heavy person in the saddle will invariably slow down the speed of a horse. Thus, there is something for everyone in sports and there is something for anyone interested in the Chinese martial arts, no matter what his physical dimensions might be. To find out what style would be "best" for the would-be student, he must assess his own physique and examine its capabilities. Then he should find the proper system most suited to his body.

In old China, masters went so far as to organize fighting styles to adapt their bodies to the terrain. If the geographic area was mostly wet, snowy or muddy, close-in hand-fighting techniques were stressed. Crowded seaport cities, such as Shanghai, in Southern China, also saw the development of close proximity seizing and grappling styles. Chin Na became the best known of the close-quarter styles. If the location was flat and dry, as in Northern China, that meant that there was more room for free fighting. Based on the generalization that Northern Chinese tended to be taller than their brothers in Southern China, leg techniques were emphasized, such as the Northern Shaolin system's high jump kicks and low extended leg sweeps, to bring down one or more upright aggressors. In rocky and rugged regions, low horse balance stances were learned along with running, jumping and shifting moves over uneven terrain. These are exemplified in the Monkey style.

Maintaining that there is no "best" system, we say that all styles have something to offer to the martial arts. Since all styles depend on speed, power, accuracy, timing and feinting maneuvers, all systems can be equally effective if performed by a master of genuine ability.

Many ancient masters concluded that almost all styles in their most advanced forms were actually quite similar to each other. They felt that not more than thirty techniques were necessary for advanced defensive training. If the disciple could master only ten techniques and apply just one of them perfectly in combat, he could succeed. That means when we get right down to the basics it is the practitioner himself who counts, not the system. As long as the proponent of any known style has acquired precision balance and lightning co-ordination of his learned hand and foot movements, he will be capable of successfully defending himself against any other stylist. In the end, it is the man and his own developed talent that will determine the outcome of physical conflict.

With so many styles to choose from and with undoubtedly new ones yet to be developed, the talented student still should study the most appropriate system to complement his body and personality. In the previous chapter we mentioned the most popular of the internal or "soft" styles, such as T'ai Chi Ch'uan. In this chapter we would like to present a representative selection of the "hard" or external styles, some well known, some fairly obscure, but each containing its own particular advantage.

This brief sampler is offered as another taste of encouragement for the reader to look more into the martial arts of China, the home of the greatest variety of self-defense styles in the history of the world.

NORTHERN SHAOLIN

Shaolin, signifying the greatest of the temple boxing systems, continues to be recognized as the most famous name of all the external Chinese martial arts, although not necessarily the most popular of the "hard" forms today.

With the original Shaolin Temple in Northern China long since destroyed, the main branches of Shaolin Kung Fu spread far and wide through China, undergoing many revisions and adaptations. The present system, known as Northern Shaolin, specializes in long-range fighting techniques. Based on some of the original temple boxing heritage, the proponents of this system maintain that kicks are more effective than hand movements because the legs obviously are longer than the arms. Thus, a master would not have to be any closer than a leg's length away from any opponent to stay in striking distance. He can dart in aggressively, kick his target and instantly withdraw, whereas a Southern Shaolin stylist, depending more on hand techniques, will stand his ground in a powerfully deep horse stance waiting for an attack. However, the Northerner, generally taller than the Southerner, utilizes his longer leg advantage by employing every kick known to martial arts.

The four basic kicks, whether aimed high or low, use the heel, the toe and the side and ball of the foot. Another basic is the stabbing kick to counter an opposing kicking attack. Low horse stances are not overly emphasized because the Northern Shaolin adept is moving all the time. His legs propel a constant flow of spins, twists and sweeps, sometimes in a complete circle. Leg scissor moves, front and back flips along with somersaults complement a stunning acrobatic performance. Some of the circular kicks are certainly quite spectacular. While spinning 360 degrees in the air, a Northerner is able to unleash the double threat roundhouse kick and the back roundhouse kick, all in a single leap. With all of these circular gyra-

功氣演表章汝術非是最考國次一第館術國央中長社術國州廣

Grand Master Lung Chi Cheung, under the wheel of a 1930 car, displays how Ch'i Kung power may protect the stomach. The Chinese caption says "The Central Martial Arts Association [run by the government] has selected Lung Chi Cheung to be the Grand Master of the Canton Martial Arts Studio. Lung was selected the number one Master of Ch'i Kung in the first national competition."

Northern Shaolin Master Lung Kai Ming, during one of his many exhibitions of Ch'i Kung, demonstrates his art to a youthful gathering aboard a boat in Hong Kong Harbor. Master Lung placed five bricks on top of his head. His brother, using a sledge hammer, broke the bricks. Master Lung emerged uninjured.

Master Lung, with his students atop a Hong Kong building, practices a back leaning horse stance for grace and co-ordination. This exercise develops strong leg sweeping power. The hands are shown in a movement borrowed from the crane; the right hand with a wing block, the left poised for a pecking attack.

The forward block and punch are a basic combination which must be mastered by Northern Shaolin students. Master Lung tells the class to overextend the tendons during practice for the body to "achieve its maximum potential."

tions going on nonstop, the antagonist tends to get confused or bewildered while trying to figure out where the next blow will come from as the Northern Shaolin expert executes his graceful, even flowery movements which are literally beautiful to behold in their almost ballet-like loveliness. However, do not misinterpret a "soft" or gentle appearance as a lack of strength. Concealing his power source well within the whirlwind of his motion, the master may set up the opponent and explode his attack at any selected fraction of a second with the outgoing blow usually never seen but always felt.

The Northern Shaolin defensive positions stress that a student should never face an aggressor head-on, rationalizing that there would be more area to protect. Instead, face him sideways with the arms extended defensively toward him. Arms extended sideways also are able to reach just a little farther than they can when standing straight in front of an opponent. In addition, there is the advantage that the shoulder offers another barrier and more distance away from any head blow or midsection striking attempts. That extra inch or so might mean the difference between life, serious injury or even death.

One of the respected Northern Shaolin masters in Hong Kong is a Catholic who instructs hundreds of youths at the Wong Tai Shin Community Center in the crown colony. Thirty-seven-year-old Lung Kai Ming learned the art as a ten-year-old boy from his father, Lung Chi Cheung, when they lived in Kwangchow, China. His father's sifu was Kou Yu Chung, a famous Northern Shaolin stylist and master of Ch'i Kung, inner power. This heritage has been passed on to the younger Sifu Lung. He is often asked to give demonstrations of his inner power (see photos), which traditionally has been an integral part of Shaolin training. Sifu Lung says he instructs his students to kick as high as possible and stretch the body muscles and tendons as far as possible in practice. He says that "the body should be trained to achieve its maximum potential. You may never be forced to use an extremely high kick to the top of an opponent's head, but merely acquiring that tremendous suppleness in your body will be benefit enough to your health." In his emphasis of leg power, Sifu Lung says many other kinds of stylists used to come to his kwoon (training hall) seeking a personal demonstration or contest. He says he would usually oblige them and "just use my legs to discourage their advances." The sifu says that his students are taught the basic leg work along with hand grabbing, clawing, hitting and blocking techniques, then they move into the long and rather complex forms of the Northern Shaolin style, including the dazzling Northern weapon sets. While all weapons are studied intensely for timing, control and speed, the long staff and spear are the ones mostly highlighted for long-range fighting. The versatile long staff, carried inoffensively anywhere, was always a favorite Shaolin "pole weapon." The spear goes back in Shaolin history when it was used to fight on horseback. Labeled the "King of Weapons," the spear was used as an offensive powerhouse for slashing, poking, jabbing, sweeping and, of course, ultimately, for throwing. (Because of its suppleness, Chinese rattan wood was used to make spears. Rattan spears could be flexibly whipped back and forth or circularly to simultaneously block and cut an opponent.) And concerning some of the Shaolin mythology, Sifu Lung says that he believes the legend that the Northern Shaolin style was brought from the original Shaolin Temple in Honan Province to the "Shaolin Temple" on Sung San Mountain in Fukien some four hundred years ago during the Ming dynasty. Whether that unauthenticated story is true is not really a pressing historical issue these days, with the authentic Northern Shaolin system itself continuing to be a vital part of the Chinese martial arts, especially suited for those with long and fast legs.

DRAGON

The mythical dragon has been characterized in the West as a serpentlike, winged monster which, according to some religions, including Christianity, represents the power of evil. The Dragon of the Apocalypse (Revelation, Chapter 12) gave rise to the use of the fire-breathing beast in Christian literature and art as a symbol of Satan. In medieval legend, the highest achievement of a hero was the slaying of a dreaded dragon. The six-thousand-line Anglo-Saxon poem *Beowulf* perhaps best exemplified this popular Western folklore. This great poem describes the heroic Gothic warrior, Beowulf, who slew the monster Grendel, which had been ravaging and wasting the land. However, other cultures, especially the Chinese, believed that the fabulous creature was benevolent, life-giving and worthy of reverence, indeed, even worship. In the words of the insightful *I Ching*, "In due time Man makes his appearance and sets about his work, like the Dragon on wing in the heavens, his beneficent influence spreads over the world."

The Chinese dragon symbolized earth and water. During the Celestial Empire it was the emblem for the imperial family, with the "Son of Heaven" often referred to as the "Dragon King" (Lung Wang). The dragon represented the sagacious protector of the land despite the fact that it also typified the destructive aspect of water and nature generally. The imperial dragon was depicted with five hawklike claws, with the more common variety shown with four talons.

In ancient China, the dragon, as a Yang force, was associated with male fertility (the jade gem stone was thought to have come from the congealed semen of the dragon). Above all, the dragon represented the fertilizing power of rain. As the continuous pelts of rain may be used for healthy

growth, they may also be used to engulf or destroy as in the Dragon style
of Kung Fu. The Ch'an Buddhists at the Shaolin Monastery felt that the
dragon meant even more than the harbinger of rain or the sign of royalty.
The auspicious creature was a cosmic manifestation that signified the
momentary, elusive vision of enlightened Truth which is eventually and
suddenly realized by a Ch'an master. To the Taoists, the dragon epitomized the Tao itself, an all-consuming force that may suddenly reveal itself to us only to instantly disappear and leave us wondering if the flash of
revelation was all a dream. Okakura Kakuzo, in *The Awakening of Japan*
(1906), wrote this provocative interpretation of the oriental dragon:
"Hidden in the caverns of inaccessible mountains or coiled in the un-
fathomable depths of the sea, he awaits the time when he slowly rouses
himself to activity. He unfolds himself in the storm clouds; he washes
his mane in the blackness of the seething whirlpools. His claws are in the
forks of the lightning, his scales begin to glisten in the bark of rain-swept
pine trees. His voice is heard in the hurricane which, scattering the
withered leaves of the forest, quickens the new spring. The dragon reveals
himself only to vanish."

This fierce but protective divinity became the symbol of one of the five
major branches of Shaolin Temple boxing. Shaolin nun Wu Mui, who is
said to have originated the Dragon style, was one of the last members of
the temple before its first burning and destruction in A.D. 1570 as related
by modern Dragon style historians. The Dragon self-defense heritage has
since been refined into Northern and Southern systems. In Hong Kong the
Southern style headquarters is the Dragon Sign Athletic Association, Ltd.,
which is supervised by seventy-six-year-old Grand Master Lam Kwun
Quon.[1] His forefathers developed the Dragon style seven generations after
Wu Mui devised the rudiments at the Shaolin Temple. According to Sifu
Lam his master teacher was his own father, Lam Yiu Quai, who died in
Hong Kong in 1964. He was ninety-three. The senior Lam had learned the
Dragon art from Dai Jo, a monk master. Dai Jo had received his training
from monk Master Loh Fao San at the Wah Sao Toh Monastery in
Kwangtung, Southern China. Sifu Lam's family is continuing the dragon
martial arts heritage. His number-one son is a fifty-nine-year-old Hong Kong
police sergeant who practices the art regularly. (Hong Kong police study

[1] According to British legal statute in the crown colony, every organized martial
arts style must be registered under corporate law to become legitimately recognized.
This might be a good method for ensuring the legitimacy of Western martial arts
schools where some unrecognized and illegitimate "masters" denigrate the true art
for financial gain and, in the end, discourage potential students from further training.
Better legal sanctions must be imposed here in the West to get rid of the phony
"teacher" and the bad name he is giving the arts.

Lam Kwun Quon, the seventy-two-year-old Dragon grand master from Hong Kong, demonstrates the classic Dragon crouch. This position is called Sam Tung, a basic blocking technique with the hands appearing like the claws of the mythical dragon. The eyes look directly outward without eyeball movement no matter how much the head moves around.

Grand Master Lam demonstrates the Bui Gim movement, "Carrying Sword on Back of Shoulders." The left hand blocks the attack. The right back fist is released in the form of drawing a sword from the back. Strike in a forward motion.

The Joy Mor movement, "Following-Touching," depends on pursuit of the opponent. Press or chase him with arms raised in defense, no matter how fast the antagonist is moving away. Follow up with a Chung Choy, "Rushing Punch," meaning Chinese uppercut.

The Mor Cup, "Touching-Covering" stance. Grand Master Lam says that a practitioner should sink low, stand still and fight with the hands. Drop the shoulders and bend the elbows as the opponent's blow is accepted. The Dragon master should "touch" and deflect the attempted hit with one hand. The other hand should "cover" the offending arm with a paralyzing shock hit.

A friendly gathering at the studio of Hong Kong's Dragon Sign Athletic Association. (LEFT TO RIGHT) Co-author David Chow; Chan Hon Chung, the chairman of the Hong Kong Chinese Martial Arts Association; co-author Richard Spangler; Grand Master Lam Kwun Quon; Dragon Masters Chow Fook and Chun Cheung.

many styles of Kung Fu with the Chin Na restraining and subduing techniques quite popular.) Sifu Lam also says that he has a daughter who studies her family's inherited martial art. She lives in Kwangchow, Canton, where at least thirty thousand Chinese reportedly practice the Southern Dragon style. The Hong Kong association statistics indicate that over ten thousand students currently practice the art in the crown colony.

"The Southern Dragon system," explains Sifu Lam, "features many big zig-zag movements which resemble the imagined actions of the fabled Dragon since no one ever actually saw one of these creatures. Advance-attack and retreat-protect techniques are performed with the practitioner constantly extending and contracting his body." The Dragon specialty at the time of attack is a combination of Hard and Soft techniques. Exponents rely on "floating and sinking movements with shoulders dropped and elbows bent." A powerful outflow of thrusting power is then released, for example, with waist-high snap kicks which may be compared with the sharp slams of a dragon's tail. A Dragon stylist defends himself by withdrawing or curving his body inwardly to absorb or neutralize any incoming punch. By withdrawing during an attack, the Dragon master will retaliate only when the adversary has overreached himself. The defender's movements, like those of the undulating great serpent, are unceasing, confusing to the assailant, and deny an opening for any decisive blow. He uses the hands to block strikes to the head or upper body. Grasping and twisting limbs are emphasized for one hand, with the other always ready as an offensive weapon.

There is also a hissing-like "dragon" sound that is emitted during concentrated breathing and focusing of strength. This sound may be likened to the sniffing and puffing of the Western boxer who incorporates proper breathing with the release of his punches to get maximum power. The "dragon" hiss helps to provide the same kind of total efficient use of the body. The main rule is never execute a striking technique while inhaling a great amount of air, i.e., do not breathe in heavily while punching outward.

With lungs filled to capacity, the impact of a blow could be injurious to the one who delivered it. The reverberation of the shock wave through the body from the hard impact of any of the limbs could harm the taut lungs, with the possibility of bursting or collapsing like a punctured balloon. Therefore, always release air in the lungs as the punch makes impact with the target. This combination ensures a fully focused flow of outward force.

The Dragon fighting forms have been considered simple, even primitive, by some martial artists. However, if we take simple or primitive to mean that which is unmixed or undistorted, still retaining its natural qualities, then the Dragon style may be thought of as a basic fighting art of beauteous grace and all-surpassing efficacy. As Sifu Lam expressed the Southern Dragon style's motto:

> *Control yourself, let others do what they will.*
> *This does not mean that you are weak.*
> *Control your heart, obey the principles of life.*
> *This does not mean that others are stronger.*

WHITE CRANE

The regal spirit of the white crane has inspired what may be considered as the most elegantly beautiful of all the Chinese Kung Fu systems. Patterned after the aesthetic essence of the statuesque wading bird found mostly in marshes and open plains, the classic White Crane self-defense forms contain an unexpected deadly beauty, especially devastating for the aggressive beholder. According to the White Crane (Pak Hok) Athletic Federation in Hong Kong, this spectacular school of boxing was introduced to middle and Southern China as recently as one hundred forty years ago after being secretly developed in Tibet during the Ming dynasty. Chinese folklore relates that some five hundred years ago Ordartor, a Tibetan lama, was peacefully meditating next to a small lake not far from his

The solid foundation of White Crane footwork ensures elusiveness. Since physical blocks are not emphasized, leg maneuvers are used to sidestep an incoming force with a long-range fist response to an unprotected point.

The long-range fist, Chang Ch'uan, is a distinctive feature of White Crane requiring speed and power, which is generated from the waist. The blows are co-ordinated to conclude a violent confrontation with a single punch while disdaining hard physical blocks or parries against an opponent.

mountainside lamasery when his tranquil contemplation was harshly inter-rupted by the trumpeting and grunting of a white crane and a huge ape en-gaged in fierce combat. The lama observed that the ape, with its massive muscles, expected to easily crush the graceful, spindle-legged creature. The tailless primate charged into the crane attempting an immediate kill. How-ever the tall bird managed to evade the potentially overwhelming on-slaught. The crane continually maneuvered its body away from the grasp-ing grip of the advancing ape. Exhibiting perfect composure, the crane, using its short but powerful wings for balance and evasion movements,

The famous and regal Crane stance with hands overhead in pecking position ready to strike. The White Crane philosophy considers it unworthy of one's esteem to physically grapple with an opponent. Therefore, should a strike miss the mark, the Crane stylist will instantly retreat and set up another attack rather than jump in and wrestle with the antagonist. This technique may be compared with a bullfighter evading the charge of the bull while placing the banderillas in its neck.

In noting the long legs of the white crane, this style is particularly suited for tall, long-legged practitioners. Legs are trained for the highest possible kicks as demonstrated by forty-one-year-old White Crane sifu Ngai Yoh Tong, of Hong Kong. Observe the outstretched arms emulating a crane's wings for proper balance.

began to react to the repeatedly strong charges by unleashing its long-necked pecking power. With a rapier-like beak longer than its head the bird was endowed with a formidable weapon. Concentrating on head shots, the crane poked at the most vulnerable points to discourage the ape's awesome-appearing attack. The bird would alternately avoid the ape's rush and counter with stinging long-range blows with its sharp-pointed bill. The ape, after losing an eye, finally retreated and escaped into the trees as the crane returned unruffled to its nest to resume the protection of its eggs.

After witnessing this amazing confrontation, Ordartor became fascinated with the light feathery crane which had subdued the tremendous brute strength of the ape. Armed with his knowledge of other temple fighting arts, he became obsessed with the idea of incorporating the crane's lithe adroitness and artistic execution of maneuvers into a humanized combat system. After much trial and error, Ordartor perceived principles which could be adapted to human physical actions. He created eight fundamental techniques based on the naturally flowing movements of the crane's pecking, clawing and wing flapping reactions to attack. In addition, he adapted some of the ape's steady footwork and strong grabbing methods. By combining these with his previous martial arts training, he devised an innovative style. Initially, Ordartor labeled it the "Lion's Roar" system. Several generations and many refinements later, Tibetan monks renamed the by then complex and systematized forms Pak Hok Ch'uan, the "White Crane Fist." The current vice-chairman of the White Crane Athletic Federation in Hong Kong, Ngai Yoh Tong, relates that the Tibetan lamas eventually agreed to share their self-defense secrets with the imperial bodyguards of the Emperor and Empress of China. They decided that the crane's majestic maneuvers were well suited for the protection of Chinese royalty. Subsequently, another Tibetan lama, Sing Lung, traveled over the mountains into Kwangtung Province. He brought with him a "complete" long-range White Crane style, complete because it incorporated short hand techniques, along with internal and soft sets into the system. The lama master attracted many would-be disciples. The supreme secrecy of the White Crane art was slowly being lifted.

The main principles of the White Crane style are really quite simple and direct, although extremely difficult to perfect. Sifu Ngai explains that "We never fend off or wrestle with an attacker if we can avoid it. We rather prefer to remain in a state of perpetual motion constantly ready to snatch the right moment to attack and subdue." The sifu says that there are four main points to remember: to Hurt, to Evade, to Penetrate, and to Intercept.

TO HURT:

A White Crane master will never fight unless it is to save lives or prevent harm to others. This includes, of course, the protection of oneself from destruction. Therefore, during a combat situation, he will be compelled to hurt an assailant up to the point when the opponent voluntarily gives up his aggression. Should the master have no intention of subduing the aggressor, he himself might be seriously injured or killed. Many boxers have been unnecessarily harmed in the past because their protective actions were lax. They were immediately taken advantage of by the adversary after a lackadaisical or unfocused response. If a fight is unavoidable, an absolutely positive and totally determined effort is required to overcome a potentially stronger force. A White Crane stylist does not hold back. Following an attacker's first sign of aggression, the White Crane master will then himself become the persistent aggressor. An instantaneous and nonstop attacking spirit is mandatory for the White Crane stylist.

TO EVADE:

The White Crane master almost haughtily disdains physical contact with an opponent, instead opting for a single debilitating blow, usually delivered from long range. A White Crane saying has it that "If you evade an attack, there will only be one attack; if you block an attack there will be ten attacks." This means that although an opponent's combative charge might be extremely forceful, should he miss his target entirely in the first attack, his momentum will carry him off balance as he catches only air. He will be unable to unleash an immediate second attack while the White Crane master will be poised to deliver a crushing strike to the weakest point of the assailant. On the other hand, if one physically blocks an attacker's arm or leg, the opponent will not necessarily be knocked off balance. He might make use of the block to stabilize himself against the White Crane master's body and launch a lightning-fast follow-up attack. With balance sustaining blocks there could be more than ten attacks coming in one after the other. Thus, "To evade is better than to block an attack."

TO PENETRATE:

This means to break through the defense of the adversary. The master should take advantage of the tense side of the opponent's attention or the lax side of his inattention. Launch a strike from an unexpected direction. Strike an unexpected area. White Crane penetration may be defined as "attacking when the assailant exposes an area of weakness." Crushing the weakness will crush the opponent.

TO INTERCEPT:

Violent situations could possibly arise in which distasteful physical contact might be forced by a strong opponent. Sifu Ngai says there are some basic methods of intercepting and responding to an attack. "There is a 'physical interception' where a blow is intercepted just as it is launched. The arm or leg may be seized or stopped from reaching its intended destination on the Master's body. The Master may then follow with an instantaneous counterattack." White Crane stylists prefer to avoid grabbing actions but, as these are a part of the total system, they may call upon the use of these techniques in an emergency. In another example, Sifu Ngai says that "If an adversary attacks from the east, the Master may seize him and take him to the west, his action will be neutralized; or if an opponent attacks from the front, the Master may take him towards his own back and topple him. This is 'negative interception,' i.e., the application of pressure in the same direction as the antagonistic force." So, if need be, hands and legs may be used to grab or block an onrushing attacker. But while the attacker may be thwarted in his forward movement, Sifu Ngai says, "The Master will always move forward into the opponent's retreating motion and put the pressure on him again and again." This exemplifies the White Crane fighting spirit of continuous movement, continuous attack.

In White Crane boxing, the force of any motion "is as indistinguishable as still water" despite the fact that when it is exerted with focused energy a dynamic power will result. This is known as "surge motion." It may be likened to the incoming and outgoing of the ocean waves on a beach. The White Crane master's arms swing in and out with power generated from the waist, pounding like the waves, flowing incessantly. The swinging arms, like battering rams, alternate. As one arm strikes forward, the other is readied in back almost in the sense of a pulley being used to increase the physical advantage of an applied force. The fists transmit the force engendered by the power from the body through the arms. Contending that there must be a totally free flow of force, there is no snapping of the wrist or fist in White Crane. The thought is that any snapping would interrupt the already turned-on current of power. This rhythmic waist and arm turning not only maximizes power and reach, it minimizes the White Crane master's target area, i.e., it puts more distance between him and the attacker.

As a traditionally long and complex Kung Fu system, the White Crane's legacy is not flourishing as it should. Sifu Ngai suggests that the speedy pace of this century might force a condensation of the ancient forms. For example, there are approximately one thousand movements contained in the ten standard weapons sets. Perfection of these forms takes enormous concentration coupled with more than just a few years' time. It would take fifteen years to absolutely master the fourteen hand sets plus the ten weapons sets. Consideration is now being given to eliminate some of the repeated movements in efforts to produce shorter, more "economical" forms. However, the traditional masters continue to argue against any dilution of their so highly respected White Crane heritage. Should a student grasp the incomplete art too quickly without proper care, the White Crane style could prove to be ineffectual and ultimately meaningless, its natural elegance hidden. Thus, a dilemma is posed—Adapt to modern times and lower the precisely conceived high standards or slowly lose the essence of the White Crane art because of lack of dedicated interest. Tradition versus reform. It is to be hoped that the White Crane community will find the harmonious answer to avoid extinction.

WING CHUN

While the American Revolution was spawning the United States in 1776, a woman in China was giving birth to a revolutionary fighting form of Kung Fu. Yim Wing Chun, a pretty young lady betrothed to Leong Bok Chao, was being pressured into breaking her engagement and marrying an infamous Yunan Province rogue. This local gang leader told her and her father that if she said "no," there would be grim consequences to the family. Ng Mui, a nun who had escaped from the destroyed Shaolin Temple, heard about these threats and suggested to Wing Chun's father that he send a letter to her fiancé, living in Fukien Province, asking that he break the engagement. Then Ng Mui said because of the great distance for the letter to travel in those perilous times that the newly planned wedding should be postponed for one year. Wing Chun's father told the rich ruffian of this proposal and he immediately agreed. But what he didn't know was that the entire plan was a delaying tactic to put off the marriage. Then Ng Mui took Wing Chun to her Pah Noh Temple and privately instructed her in Shaolin fighting techniques, using her own ingenious female modifications. (Nuns were proficient in Kung Fu, with some of these shaven-headed holy women purportedly unbeatable in competition.) This Buddhist nun told Wing Chun that with diligent daily training she could learn the necessary fundamentals to defend herself within twelve months. Realizing the crucial circumstances, Wing Chun practiced every possible moment under the gifted guidance of Ng Mui.

The year passed. Ng Mui then had Wing Chun's father inform the town troublemaker that his daughter had studied Kung Fu since childhood and would only marry someone who could defeat her in hand-to-hand combat. Boastfully beaming with overconfidence, the hopeful bridegroom, who claimed to be a fighter himself, set the showdown in the town square for all to see. He aggressively charged at Wing Chun. She knocked him down. Getting up, he came at her harder. She hit him harder. Every time he tried to attack her with more force, the harder she hit him. He finally realized that his classical brute strength block and punch style was no match for Wing Chun's simple and direct aggressive technique. In efforts to save a little "face," he and members of his gang quickly left, shouting threats of revenge. A relieved but thoughtful Ng Mui took the happy Wing Chun to the remote Kwon How Temple in Kwangtung Province, where the bully would not bother her anymore. She continued to teach the talented Wing Chun, who began to categorize her learning into three practical empty-hand forms: Siu Lim Tao, "A Little Thought"; Tzum Kiu, "Searching for the Opponent's Opening"; Biu Gee, "Shooting Fingers." Ng Mui, sensing the greatness of her first disciple, named this developing style in her honor. Thus "Wing Chun" (meaning "Glorious Springtime") began to bloom. Also Wing Chun's love life flowered. She married her true love, Leong Bok Chao, and, being a good wife, taught him all of Wing Chun. Leong became a master with many talented students, among them a rich merchant, Leung Lan Kwai, in Kwan Sai, Canton, and Wong Wah Bo, a wardrobe man in a traveling opera. Wong's close friend, Leung Yee Tai, was a master of the Shaolin six-and-a-half-point staff techniques. Wong and Leung Yee Tai exchanged techniques, leading to the eventual inclusion of staff training in Wing Chun. It was during the performance of the opera in Fut Shan that Leung Yee Tai, becoming ill, went to Dr. Leung Tzan. Dr. Leung, amazed by Leung Yee Tai's prowess in Wing Chun, asked to be accepted as a disciple. After determined training, Dr. Leung stood up to many challenges, undefeated in fierce competition where only the winner was able to walk away; while the loser was not necessarily dead he was usually seriously injured. It was because of Leung Tzan's heralded fighting reputation that the Wing Chun style became famous in the Southern Chinese Kung Fu circles.

Historically, we can call Ng Mui the originator, Wing Chun, herself, the organizer, and Leung Tzan the promoter. Leung then taught the art to

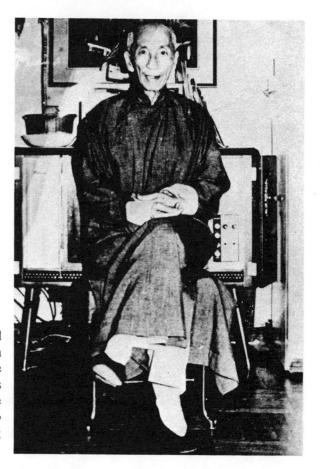

The late Yip Man, who was the venerated leader of the Wing Chun Athletic Association in Hong Kong. He was a great believer in the heritage of China. Grand Master Yip was saddened by any encroachment on Chinese tradition. But before his death he managed to accept some modern advantages, including the television set behind him.

Chan Wah Soon, who instructed the late Yip Man, the respected leader of the Wing Chun clan in Hong Kong. This mild-mannered master was seventy-eight when he died of throat cancer in 1973. While small in stature (five feet five), Sifu Yip was silently an imposing figure of a man with definite opinions. For instance, he did not like to pose for publicity photographs, he never wore Western clothes, and he felt that only Chinese should be taught Wing Chun to maintain its purity. This last injunction is changing slowly as a few Americans are studying Wing Chun in Hong Kong under some of Yip's leading disciples, Leung Sheung, Lok Yu, Tsui Sheung Tin, and Wong Soon Leong.

Most Wing Chun masters presently feel that they do not have anything really to hide and that the "goodness" of their art should be spread to the West. The essence of Wing Chun, in Chinese terms, is "Opponent attacks, absorb and neutralize blow. Opponent withdraws, pursue and counter. Disengage restriction from arms, retaliate with penetrating thrust." This will take some thought to understand and a lot of practical application to master. Technically, Wing Chun uses a constant flow of forward energy

Thirty-five-year-old Wing Chun Master Po Kin Wah (LEFT), a Hong Kong English teacher, practices Chi Sao with a student. This "Sticky Hands" technique must be mastered for true Wing Chun proficiency.

Wing Chun Master Po constantly practices on the Sha Dip, a punching bag filled with steel beebees. He trains to focus jarring punches from varying distances, the shorter the better. An effective blow can be obtained from six inches, sometimes less. The late Bruce Lee, a Wing Chun exponent, practiced a one-inch punch known to be lethal.

The right hand is released from an on-guard position near the center of his chest. Master Po snaps his wrist straight to the target. Note the knuckle action. The Wing Chun master uses all four knuckles for hitting, with special emphasis on the bottom three.

The prescribed defensive-offensive movements of the Muk Jong (Wooden Dummy) are performed with instant fluid motion.

This is a typical stance of directly facing an opponent and delivering a kick to the kneecap.

High kicks are rarely delivered in Wing Chun. Masters maintain that low kicks, those below the waist, are safer for the practitioner while providing an effective means of subduing an opponent. Leg sweeps and stomps may be used.

based on the principle that the shortest distance between two points is a straight line. For example, should your opponent throw a hook punch at the precise instant that you release your straight punch, your blow obviously will land first, since it travels a shorter distance. Offensively, a Wing Chun artist will use a combination of straight and intercepting lines and deflectings arcs. We emphasize the word "offense" because Wing Chun is structurally an aggressive close-quarter style which, as a modern Wing Chun practitioner told us, "Doesn't give a damn about traditional block and punch routines."

Chi Sao—the Way to Wing Chun Proficiency

Wing Chun can be mastered only by the diligent practice of Chi Sao, which we interpret as the art of "Tenacious Hands." Others have termed it as "Sticky Hands." It has been described as a "psychophysical" training in which two practitioners place their two outstretched hands together and then try to penetrate each other's defensive circle. The hands should be quietly alive, that is, soft and supple but unyielding; forceful and firm but not hard or inflexible. Leading Wing Chun masters stress that Chi Sao should not be thought of as a combat system. It is, rather, a specialized training method designed to maximize the total efficiency of Wing Chun. In addition to Wing Chun's three empty-hand sets, there are only three other training forms: the 108 or 116 movements of the wooden dummy (Muk Jong); the eight slashing techniques of the butterfly sword (Pah Tsam Tao) and, the techniques of the six-and-a-half-point staff (Lok Dim Poon Kwam). Wing Chun is a simple, compact system, devoid of sophisticated sets of a thousand moves. A talented novice can acquire adequate self-defense ability within one year, just as Wing Chun did.

HUNG GAR CH'UAN

The five most prominent individually developed Kung Fu systems found in Southern China are known by their family names, Hung, Lau, Choi, Lee and Mok. Among these "gar" (meaning family or clan) styles, Fukien tea merchant Hung Hei Goon became the best known of the group with a two-hundred-year-old reputation as "The Southern Fist." Hung Gar Ch'uan is an adaptation of the Shaolin Tiger system originally taught to Hung by the monk Master Jee Seen, according to legend, at the Shaolin Temple in Fukien. Master Jee's initial instruction stressed close-quarter fighting methods. The stances were only fourteen inches wide. Four square feet would be enough room to perform an entire "set." His system was totally unlike the far-ranging jumping styles of the North, but it was extremely effective for combat in the confining alleys of China during the Ch'ing dynasty. Some streets were so narrow that they could not accept even the passage of a rickshaw or sedan chair. It could be compared to fighting in a twentieth-century clothes closet. Eventually, after a thorough observation of the existing Kung Fu styles, Master Jee modified his system for broader application in a balance of long- and short-range techniques.

Disciple Hung took his subsequent mastery of the Tiger Claw and combined it with his wife's White Crane style expertise which featured graceful finger curl hooking and sharp pecking actions.[2] He further added to his

[2] Hung Hei Goon was married to Fong Wing Chun, who studied the white Crane system also under the tutelage of Master Jee Seen. Wing Chun (no relation to Yim Wing Chun) learned the art to avenge the murders of her entire family, slaughtered by bandits.

personal adaptation by using selected techniques of the Dragon, Leopard and Snake forms. Hung also included aspects of the "Five Element Fists": metal, for strong hammer and back fist; wood, for simultaneous blocking and punching; water, for a series of battering blows as the ocean waves ceaselessly pound the shore; fire, for rapid, straight strikes as in a bombardment of rockets; and earth, destructive blows to vital body cavities resulting in a cave-in of total annihilation. The Chinese "Five Element Fist" technique remains rare today. Although it is the backbone of at least one style, Hsing I, the easiest to learn of the three internal fighting systems.

Speciality of Hung Gar

Ancient Hung Gar Ch'uan practitioners, famed for their calm and uncomplaining endurance, began their training as novices by standing in low horse stances while practicing straight punches. They did this for three burnings of incense sticks every day for three years before learning any advanced techniques. (One incense stick lasted approximately one hour.) Modern training, however, is not as grueling. In Hong Kong, for example, Hung Gar artists considered a half hour in the strong horse stance adequate for daily exercise, in addition to the practice of powerful boxing and weapons sets. Special techniques include "a tremendous thrust punch," which, according to Hung Gar contention, always results in a knockout from a single blow (with proper application, of course). The Tiger Claw, Seven Star Slashing Blows, knife hand, groin kick, and side kick are other distinctive features. The most famous followers of Hung Gar Ch'uan are Tit Kiu Saam, Lam Fook Sing, Wong Kei Ying, his son, Wong Fei Hung (the fighting master made famous in modern Chinese movies starring Kwan Tak Hing), and Lam Sai Wing. The current leading figures in Hong Kong are Chan Hon Chung, Lum Jo, Ho Lap Tien, and Mok Yee. The art is now spreading slowly to the United States, especially Hawaii and California.

Should this powerful Hung Gar style sound appealing, you must understand its basic moral principles, which promulgate honesty and righteousness, chivalry and an iron willpower. Even the surname "Hung" means to stand tall with integrity. Hung Gar Ch'uan has epitomized Buddha's teaching, "He trained himself to avoid abusing others, and then he wished that all might have the serene mind that would follow in living at peace with others."

PRAYING MANTIS

The most devout-appearing insect in the world has to be the praying mantis. With its front legs commonly held in a way suggestive of hands folded in prayer, it has become the most revered insect in all of the Chinese martial arts. This brother to the grasshopper has become so venerated not because of its seeming aura of religiousness but because of its remarkable ferocity, pugnacity and tenacity of life. Some three hundred fifty years ago a fighting master, Wang Lang, exalted the little but feisty creature by creating the Praying Mantis style of self-defense. However, had it not been for a series of humiliating defeats suffered by Wang, the mantis (from the Greek word for diviner or prophet) might have been overlooked or ignored. Praying Mantis Master Chao Tsu Tse tells us that Wang Lang had been a superior swordsman who thought himself to be invincible, despite hearing others claim that the Shaolin monks were unconquerable in the martial arts. Determined to dislodge this assertion from popular belief, Wang went to the Shaolin Temple and issued a challenge to the monk masters to test their skills against him in brotherly contest. Due to his repeated insistence, the head monk relented and permitted Wang to have his way. A novitiate monk was sent against him. To Wang's astonishment and chagrin, he was decisively defeated by the low-ranking monk. Retreating into the seclusion of the mountains, Wang was determined to prove himself to the monks.

He trained diligently in his "Way of the Sword" (T'sien Tao) style while at the same time constantly exercising and strengthening his body. He returned to the monastery convinced that he was ready to show the monks his newly attained superiority. The gracious monks again accepted his invitation to contest their skills. Again he faced the lowest monk. With a feeling of exultation he overcame the young neophyte. He defeated another low-ranking monk and yet another, of higher rank. Wang was beginning to feel his former confidence of invincibility until he faced the head monk. With the entire Shaolin order watching, Wang was unable to touch the head monk. He was soundly beaten. Again retreating with his battered body and wounded pride, Wang disappeared into the forest for contemplation. One day while resting under a tree, Wang heard the long shrill note of a cicada in the low-hanging branches just above him. Looking silently upward, Wang spotted a fragile, almost brittle-appearing praying mantis engaged in a life-or-death struggle with the heavy-bodied cicada. The cicada was slowly pushing its hard, blunt head against the mantis, nearly pinning it down with its pincers, when the mantis reacted by ferociously using his strong spiny forelegs and biting mouth to grasp the stout cicada and subdue it. The carnivorous mantis then consumed his prey. Highly impressed at what he had witnessed, Wang decided to capture the victorious insect and further observe its defensive and offensive movements. Using a short length of straw, he poked and prodded the mantis from all directions. Invariably, the mantis, with its head able to turn in any direction, defended itself effectively whether provoked from the front or back. The persevering mantis became Wang's all-consuming inspiration for a new system of combat. With meticulous care, he organized the defensive and aggressive movements of the mantis into a human fighting art. He devised three main categories: P'eng P'u, the all-important method of hitting or throwing the antagonist off balance; Lan T'seh, using, restraining or reducing an opponent's strength; and P'a Tsou, the *coup de grâce* "eight elbow" offense.

After steadfast and concentrated personal preparation he finally made up his mind that he was ready to test his newly created fighting style against the master monks. Armed with his inspired mantis moves, Wang overwhelmingly defeated the finest of the monks with his bewildering display of insect tactics never before used by man. The deferential monks, accepting defeat humbly although expressing some astonishment, sought to learn about his strange new system. Word of his victory spread through the provinces. Wang Lang was the new martial arts hero. He soon was surrounded by hundreds of disciples. Wang Lang's dream of martial arts greatness was finally realized. His Praying Mantis school of self-defense became extremely prominent in Northern China, considered by some to be the most prominent during his lifetime.

The venerable Wang died years later, a content and famous fighting master. However, his carefully thought out mantis heritage became divided during the Ch'ing dynasty when four disciples, each claiming superior innovations, sought to be released from the founding school. The Mantis master said their desires would be granted on one condition—that each disciple name his individualized system after the markings on the back of a personally captured mantis. One had the appearance of the Yin-Yang symbol (Tai T'si), another looked like a plum blossom (Mei Hua) and one set of markings showed seven apparent stars (Tsi T'sing). Then there was the mantis that had no obvious marking at all. That style was called the Bare

LEFT: The traditional Praying Mantis on-guard position, demonstrated by Grand Master Chao Tsu Tse at his Hong Kong school. Notice the hands, which resemble the fighting readiness of the insect's poised feelers. RIGHT: Grand Master Chao shows the "Seven Star" stance. The right hand is used for blocking. The left hand is utilized for poking and stabbing actions.

system (Kwong P'an). Eventually, the Yin-Yang Mantis school, founded by the gentlemanly martial artist Liang Tsu Shan, emerged as generally the more effective school. Greatly admired for his courtesy and thoughtfulness, he unstintingly honored all other martial arts schools while still actively advancing his own. He felt that there was something to be learned from all the styles. On the occasion of his eightieth birthday, Liang himself was honored by all of the recognized fighting masters in Northern China.

Seventy-five-year-old Sifu Chao Tsu Tse indicates that seven of the grand master's adopted god-brothers gave the esteemed Liang the ultimate gift of a martial artist—the precisely written and drawn principles of their best and last techniques, something they would have hesitated to give to their own disciples for fear they would be defeated by them later. Thus, their gift was a symbol of total respect for Liang. Two of the bestowed techniques—Sung Yu Tung's "Hei Kung," or enhancement of breathing method, and Suen Ke Yang's ground fighting movements—were later embodied into the official system of Yin-Yang Praying Mantis.

This one-leg side stance is highly effective for defensive and offensive movements. Grand Master Chao explains that the hands may be used to block, grab and hit. The raised leg may be used to block and kick.

Now, three generations later in the twentieth century, the dignified Sifu Chao has become the acknowledged grand master of Yin-Yang Praying Mantis. During his youth, Sifu Chao said that he started his martial arts career as a security guard for gold shipments in his native Shantung, China. He contended against many savage bandits back in the 1920s, while in recent years Sifu Chao has assisted in lessening another kind of aggression. He introduced Yin-Yang Praying Mantis to military officers in South Vietnam, where he sent one of his personally taught masters to be the bodyguard for the South Vietnamese President. With his kindly face never revealing his uncanny fighting ability, Sifu Chao explained that all the Northern Praying Mantis techniques stress that one hand should be used to defend at all times. The guarding hand is kept up and centered around the front of the face rather than at the chest or hip level, as in some other styles. The other hand should always remain free to execute the next move whether offensive or defensive. This means that two or three things are happening at once. The left hand might be seizing the antagonist's incoming left-hand punch, pulling it past his own body while smashing the opponent's rib cage with his right elbow and at the same time hooking his right leg around the aggressor's left leg to make certain he goes down. In addition to many elbow strikes and uppercut blows, there is a heavy reliance on elusive footwork. Waist high kicks are featured. The intricate and acrobatic sets designed for Praying Mantis training actually resemble the pugnacious creature. They are practiced barehanded and with weapons. The hands often assume the appearance of the fighting readiness of the insect's doubled-up forelegs with feelers poised. The fast foot techniques are patterned after the long-legged mantis hops.

The mantis has always been well thought of as one of nature's most beneficial creatures. With its long body and swivel head, it is a streamlined insect that likes to rid its domain of infesting insects that prey on life-giving vegetation. While the mantis was first used in the United States some fifty years ago to aid in the control of harmful insects, the Praying Mantis fighting system has only begun to make its welcome presence known in the past decade. May this system of defense continue to thrive for the further benefit of mankind.

MONKEY STYLE

Despite being the most comical appearing of all the martial arts, the Monkey style should not be laughed at because it is truly one of the world's most deadly personal defense systems. It traces its origins back to the time China first permitted foreign missionaries to enter the country in 1842. It seems that a Ch'ing dynasty conscription officer went to draft Kau See, a ground fighting expert, into the army. When he said, in effect, "Hell no, I won't go," the induction officer tried to take him forcibly to the Manchu military headquarters. Kau See resisted and inadvertently killed the officer. Realizing his unexpected crime, the normally peaceful Kau See surrendered himself to Peking police who put him behind bars. From his cell he could see a monkey family living in the trees surrounding the prison.[3] Eventually, in his desperation to keep physically fit and mentally alert while wallowing in confinement, he began to study and imitate the hunting and survival movements of the feisty little mammals. Kau See concentrated on their fighting techniques by picking out the group's superior monkey and repeating every move he made during conflicts with other apes or predators. This daily monkey fighting practice continued for nearly ten years until he was released from prison after officials pardoned him for his

[3] Chinese penal authorities used apes as "watchdogs." Should a prisoner manage to break out, the monkeys would sound a loud chattering alarm which would alert the Chinese army guards.

Monkey Master Chan Chiu Chung assumes a low and close-in defensive stance. The raised leg braced by the left hand may be released like a steel spring against his opponent. The poised right hand may be used for a full fist strike, a one knuckle punch, a side of the hand hit (chop) or an eye poke.

Monkey Master Chan, dropping to the hard floor of his Hong Kong studio, performs ground-rolling techniques to set up his opponent.

After seemingly meaningless rolling and spinning movements on the floor Monkey Master Chan executes a powerful kick with perfect form. This particular kick is designed for a strike to the midsection or groin.

Master Chan demonstrates a Drunken style pose by contorting his face and reeling his body as if under the influence of alcohol.

Acting the part of a "drunkard," Master Chan may stumble and fall "helplessly" to the floor, apparently at the mercy of any aggressor.

Master Chan may suddenly perform an evasive somersault, instantly "sobering up" to roll and spin toward his opponent. He is then able to unleash various kinds of thrust and wheel kicks to disable his attacker.

unpremeditated murder. He later became known as "The Monkey Master" with disciples joining him to learn his unusual hopping and squatting defense system. His training specialized in ground or close-to-the-ground techniques which required intensive leg conditioning. Students were taught to fall without harm on any hard surface, such as rocks, and, while faking with twisting and turning moves, unleash sudden precision kicks and foot sweeps. Clawing, scratching and poking hand techniques also followed the monkey manner. But Monkey stylists would never look for fights. They would rather patiently size up any possible attacker, that is, should there be time. A current Monkey sifu in Hong Kong, thirty-eight-year-old Chan Chiu Chung, says that, for example, if a tiger started to chase him, he would run for the nearest shelter. Although if he felt an opponent was controllable, he would defend himself. Even then he might run away, cunningly stop, quickly kick the pursuer and run off again.

Sifu Chan says that what must be the most diverting style in all of Kung Fu originated from the monkey. It is amusingly enough labeled "The Drunken Style." Legend has it that Monkey founder Kau See, while still in jail, saw an intoxicated man drinking near the monkey trees. In his stupor he dropped his half-filled bottle of wine, staggered away and passed out. In the "monkey see-monkey do" fashion, one of the curious apes jumped down, grabbed the bottle and gulped it down. Kau See saw the little fellow become outrageously drunk, screeching with frantic, erratic movements. Other monkeys rushed over and teasingly ganged up on him. However, even in his wobbly condition, the inebriated monkey was still able to defend himself. Kau See determined that this could be an extremely deceptive combat technique by lulling your opponent into overconfidence as he sees you stumble and reel around without apparent co-ordination. Imagine a mugger's surprise, seeing an easy mark weaving "helplessly," to be on the receiving end of the "drunkard's" full-force, perfectly planted kick to the head and groin. It is a shrewd style that is highly effective against the unsuspecting antagonist. Sifu Chan can demonstrate its inherent grace amid the outwardly clumsy appearance by holding a glass of tea in one hand and falling to the ground, performing a rapid somersault, and lashing out with accurate kicks to a target, then drink the unspilled tea.

The Monkey motto, according to the devoted sifu, is, "We are not afraid of your fist which can break rocks as long as we remain fluidly flexible and lightly elusive." His meaning can be understood if anyone has ever attempted to catch a monkey.

CHOY LEE FUT

"Maneuver the staff with the power of the dragon's slashing tail. Unleash a smashing fist as the majestic tiger instantly lifts his head at an intruder." This is the motto of Choy Lee Fut, the famous long-range rocket-punching style of Southern China which later spread to Northern China as well. It emerged from the rage of discontent in the decaying Manchurian China of the nineteenth century.

There was a small boy in Kwangtung Province who was taken by his uncle to learn the popular Hung Gar Ch'uan combat system. The youth, Chan Heung, became so eager to learn more of the martial arts that he later left his village of Chan in Gung Mui County to search for heralded Shaolin fighting masters. In the past, Shaolin monks had rarely taught their martial arts to civilians or outsiders, but after the Ch'ing government burned down their Buddhist temples the monks who survived sought refuge with those who opposed the Manchu dynasty. Some became ascetics or hermits, some became heads of small village temples, and others were absorbed into the countryside where they taught their arts to the secret rebel societies trying to overthrow the Manchus. The young Chan Heung found two Shaolin masters who advanced his training—Lee Yau San and Choy Fook. After he became a fighting master, he returned to his village and organized a secret home-town militia to resist the overbearing Ch'ing government.

One day, one of Chan's old friends, Cheung Kwon, came to visit with his nephew, Cheung Yim. Admiring Chan's fighting prowess, Cheung Kwon begged him to accept his young relative as his disciple. However, due to the rigid rules of the village elders, no outsiders were permitted to learn their secrets. Cheung Kwon then explained that the boy's parents had been killed recently and that he himself was headed on a long, perilous journey and would be unable to care for him. Acting on the accepted code of chivalry, Chan responded saying he could receive the twelve-year-old orphan into his kwoon, but only as a cleanup worker. The lad and his uncle gratefully agreed, although after several months of scrubbing, sweeping and washing, Cheung Yim became discouraged after watching the disciples train every day. He too wanted to be a fighting master. So, whenever his chores were completed and nobody was around, he secretly imitated the "sets" and moves of the students and master. Chan Heung later discovered the youngster performing his private and solo training. The sifu, sympathizing with his plight, praised the boy for his determination and taught him some lessons, secretly, of course. He was still not a home-town boy. What Chan did not realize was that he was polishing an uncut diamond. Within two years the roughness was gone.

The young man was learning the finer points of Chan's style. It happened one day that the sifu had to make an unexpected business trip to a neighboring village. The students, left without their master, began joking and playing in the kwoon. Cheung, as usual, doing the cleaning, became the butt of their jokes. Since they thought he was a weakling, they teasingly challenged him to fight. He refused. He refused again and again. But, with a limit to everything, their taunting finally got to him. He also had a deep desire to demonstrate his pugilistic talents, to find out if what he had learned through such hardship was worth the effort. In his case, the more difficult it was to acquire something the more it was to be treasured. Cheung Yim turned out to be far superior than the unbridled bunch of young disciples. Unfortunately he injured a few of them. The troublemakers went home crying to their parents. When Chan Heung returned from his brief trip, he was blamed for allowing the outsider to learn their secrets. The elders told him to expel the lonely teen-ager from the village. Reluctantly, the sifu wrote Cheung Yim a letter of introduction to become the disciple of Grand Master Ching Tzo Wo Sheun (Green Grass Monk), who had escaped from the Shaolin Temple tragedy. This imposing figure lived hidden away in the Pa Pai mountain range, not far distant from Chan Village.

Thus, in the year 1831, Cheung Yim bade farewell to Sifu Chan and continued his training, officially this time, with monk Ching Tzo. In five years the young man became a brilliant Shaolin master who was also imbued with the revolutionary spirit to topple the corrupt regime. Grand Master Ching Tzo changed Cheung's name to Hung Sing, meaning Triad Victory. The triad was a righteous revolutionary organization during this period. He was then ordered to return to Chan Village and assist his former sifu, Chan Heung, in fighting the Manchus. The newly named Hung Sing was welcomed by Sifu Chan, not as a former student, but as a younger brother, since he too had studied under monk Ching Tzo. The village elders also revaluated their opinion of the former outsider. They began to express great respect for Hung Sing, who was becoming quite renowned as a fighting master. Chan Heung and Hung Sing, in their mutual dedication to find the most effective techniques to fight the Manchus, pooled their total knowledge of martial arts and produced the system known as Choy Lee Fut. It was named in memory of Choy Fook, Lee Yau San and Ching Tzo, the ascetic monk fighting master who literally became a Buddha of enlightenment prior to his death. Fut means Buddha, thereby offering a twin homage to the grand master monk and to the religious order itself.

It is said that they first officially taught Choy Lee Fut in Gung Mui County in 1836. The village rules were changed to include outsiders. Under persistent harassment by government troops, patriotic rebels were trained in the shortest possible time. Choy Lee Fut started out as a kind of secret and emergency military combat training born out of the turmoil and horror of civil war. It is a highly aggressive system emphasizing blitzkrieg hitting attacks until the opponent is conquered. This long-range style of boxing relies heavily on elusive and deceptive foot movements. It is best known for its knuckle jabs, uppercuts, roundhouse hits, its hammer and back fist, its downward-slashing whiplike swing and the Buddhist Palm, the most advanced technique.

Choy Lee Fut's power source originates from the waist through a strong horse stance with punches released from only a foot away from the target being extremely effective. In addition to basic Chin Na grappling and throwing techniques, high and low kicks are used, side kicks, snap kicks, hook kicks and thrust kicks featuring 360-degree spins and turns. Intercepting and jamming are favorite tactics used against any enemy. Jam an opponent off balance by moving straight into him while blasting overpowering hooks and uppercuts. Some of these moves are strikingly similar to Western boxing.

Since the Manchu forces were always well armed, Choy Lee Fut guerrilla fighters, as we might call them today, also were well trained in weaponry. Their underground arsenal included the normal array of spears, tridents, halberds, lances and varying lengths and styles of chain whips, but they specialized in the long staff and broadsword. In practice, all techniques of Choy Lee Fut are extended to the utmost point in efforts to promote a well-developed physique. As Hong Kong Sifu Tsang Chiu Yu says, "Overextend your muscles in practice, while actual combat will require only one-fourth of that extension to subdue an attacker."

This whirlwind-like combat system was not shelved or discarded after the fall of the hated Manchus. Although their mission had been accomplished with the help of other historical events, Choy Lee Fut proponents

Tsang Chiu Yu (RIGHT) a thirty-eight-year-old Choy Lee Fut sifu in Hong Kong, instructs a student in the application of the low horse side-knuckle fist.

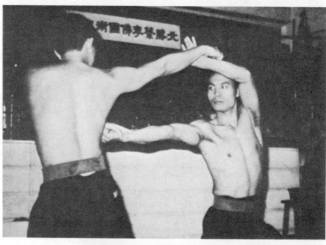

Sifu Tsang practices "Cha," hand penetration exercise, with a student.

Choy Lee Fut's famous roundhouse uppercut with left arm prepared to follow through with another one.

A side kick to the head, thought to be one of the more effective weapons in the Choy Lee Fut arsenal.

"Squat Down and Level the Beach," a movement indicating body extension, of prime concern in Choy Lee Fut practice.

Known for its different knuckle strikes, this is Choy Lee Fut's palm-up knuckle fist punch with left arm ready to block or grab any counterblow.

As an all-purpose fighting art, Choy Lee Fut uses grabbing and seizing methods, many borrowed from the popular Chin Na style of Kung Fu.

continued the art to be ever ready to fight against any future governmental corruption and oppression. Its merits have been increasingly realized during this century. Hong Kong alone has some one hundred schools of Choy Lee Fut. Taiwan has even more. The art is now spreading to Hawaii and the West Coast of the United States. The revolutionary fighting style of Choy Lee Fut, inspired by the violence of war, continues to slowly raise the veil of its past secrecy.

5.

Chin Na

Chin Na has taken a firm hold as one of the leading Chinese martial arts ever since its emergence approximately 370 years ago during the Ming dynasty. Although relatively unknown in the English-speaking world due to a lack of legitimate Chin Na masters in the West, elements of this scientifically based art are included in virtually every known system of Kung Fu. Techniques of this seizing and throwing system are utilized more than any other empty-hand self-defense style. During its 1974 tour of the United States, the Wu Shu Troupe of the People's Republic of China spotlighted Chin Na as one of the top ten "sports" of New China. The Wu Shu delegation defined the system as a "set of movements based on the method of twisting locks, including holds, counter-holds and escapes. Locks and holds are applied on the wrist, throat, elbow, neck and nerves."

Rooted in ancient wrestling and Tien'hsueh (attacking vital points), Chin Na evolved in the early 1600s, when government officials sought more restraining methods to subdue criminals without necessarily killing them. Chin Na was devised as a system of capturing and detaining. (Chin means "to capture," Na means "to hold.") As refinements were developed in the subsequent Ch'ing dynasty (A.D. 1644–1911), Chin Na became part of the basic training program for Chinese military personnel as well as province policemen. Emphasizing seizing, twisting and locking of the joints, Chin Na also employs short kicking, punching and striking techniques similar to those of many other styles of Kung Fu. The essential difference is that Chin Na does not have prescribed performance sets or long forms of movement to memorize and practice like most Chinese systems. Part of this difference is accounted for in the art's philosophy, which can be translated in the Western religious sense of "Whatever you shall sow, so shall you reap." By this admonition, a Chin Na practitioner meant that, should an opponent grab his hair, the opponent could receive a broken wrist; should an opponent's arm choke him, he could receive a broken elbow; should an opponent grab him from behind, he could receive a broken back; should the opponent attack with a knife, he could be disarmed and given a taste of his own weapon. It is the credo of the Chin Na master to conclude whatever an assailant begins. The intruder will wind up on the receiving end of his own self-initiated violence.

Chin Na combines common sense application with a physician's knowledge of anatomy, i.e., bone structure, muscle formation and all the vital areas, especially those within the nervous system. Instead of spending years perfecting a set until it becomes second nature or an instinctual part of the performer's being, the Chin Na exponent will spend his time gaining knowledge about the intricacies of the human body. He will study how muscles and bones move freely and how they may rip and break. By analyzing the entire nervous system, he learns the exact locations of the most vulnerable areas of the body. He will understand how a slight poke or press of a finger may paralyze an aggressor's arm; in turn, he will be able to restore normalcy to the limb. The Chin Na expert comprehends and acts upon the strengths and weaknesses of the body.

When two students practice Chin Na, one will always attack, the other will always defend. The defender will counter the attack until his constantly flowing techniques become offensive. The grabbing, twisting, pressing, locking and throwing moves follow one another sequentially. Should one fail, the defender moves into another subduing method. When a locking technique is unlocked by the defending partner, he must counter with an aggressive action of his own to conclude the exercise. This continuous reversal of roles lasts until one student becomes unable to defend himself.

During the latter part of the Ch'ing dynasty, Chin Na was solidly established as a major martial art of China. It had become a compulsory part of the training of every soldier and policeman. The grand master considered most responsible for the great popular emergence of Chin Na in the early years of this century was the imposing figure of Tung Tsung Nee. Born in 1880 in Wu Pei province, Grand Master Tung, a Taoist, had become a master of Chinese wrestling and Chin Na. In his late twenties, the tall and dignified Tung made his living mainly by hiring himself out as a security chief to protect caravans of merchandise which were transported from one province to another. He also acted as a bodyguard for traveling dignitaries. Acquiring a high reputation of being able to always safely deliver the goods entrusted to him, the grand master's entourages were avoided by would-be plundering outlaws. As the tumultuous toppling of the Ch'ing dynasty approached in 1910, he was appointed the Chief of Scouts for the First Chinese Combat Division. In 1912, after the birth of the Republic of China, he was promoted to be Captain of the First Combat Division's Cavalry Unit. He was also the bone and muscle specialist of the unit. With the increasing realization of his great skills, in 1918 at the age of thirty-eight, he was appointed as a leading martial arts trainer for the Chinese Army and one year later was promoted to the position of Commanding Officer of the Martial Arts Training Headquarters for the Chinese military. Grand Master Tung's military career flourished with further promotions until in 1924 he became the Commanding General of the Chinese National Guard. Three years later at the age of forty-seven he was chosen the Chief of Combat Training to oversee the martial arts instructions of cadets at the Chinese Military Academy. The military high command felt that the revered grand master should impart his invaluable self-defense knowledge to as many young military officers as possible. In 1934, General Tung retired from his illustrious military career to become the Chairman of the National Martial Arts Association, based in Shanghai. The venerable Tung Tsung Nee continued to instruct and promote self-defense arts until his death in 1971. He was ninety-one years old. The grand master had bequeathed a richly refined heritage of Chin Na to his disciples.[1] Based on his military background, he also left his favorite philosophical words to live by:

Winning the hearts is the best way.
Winning the castles is the secondary way.
Winning through domination is the worst way.

Grand Master Tung refined Chin Na into seventy-two basic restraining and subduing techniques. These methods, if perfected, could be used to neutralize any physical attack. He categorized his teaching into three general areas: 1) how to escape an opponent's striking or holding attack; 2)

[1] Among his many dedicated disciples was David Chow, who studied with the grand master for four years in Shanghai. The youthful Chow acquired his basic philosophy of life from Tung Tsung Nee—"Always measure a man's life by its depth, rather than its length."

David Chow's Grand Master Tung Tsung Nee
(1880–1971), the originator of the modern
system of Chin Na.

how to apply submission locks on the opponent; and 3) how to control an assailant through pressure on selected nerve points.

It must be emphasized that Chin Na is based on medical science. It is not a force versus force style, nor strength versus strength style. There is rather a "softness" about it. The Chin Na master will never charge into a confrontation exhibiting a furious force. His actions will certainly be swift and direct, but they will be performed with a calm, almost relaxed appearance of smoothness. Striking methods may be used following a lock or throw. Hand and leg blows are taught as part of the total system, although Chin Na specializes in locking an opponent's body in position for a limb, torso, neck or head spraining or breaking move. A follow-up strike may or may not be necessary. The most prominent exercise involves the development of the hands for seizing and holding. Sometimes referred to as "Devil's Hand" (Ti-sha Shou), the art advocates specialized hand and finger exercises, including bamboo twisting, to condition the hands. Chin Na, thought to be the grandfather of Japanese Judo and the father of Jujitsu, is the "cleanest" of the martial arts. Its perfection does not require any deforming of the body. (Some Japanese and Korean Karate schools pound and maim their hands into lethal weapons.) A Chin Na adept will hardly ever raise a callus on his hand or anywhere else on his body. Supported by practical, easy-to-practice exercises, Chin Na has become not only a part of military training but an extremely popular martial arts pastime for the weak, the small, women and children, as well as the large and strong. Chin Na may be practiced and enjoyed by anyone who has the use of two or more of his limbs.

DAVID CHOW SPEAKS TO HIS STUDENTS

A PERSONAL PHILOSOPHY

During my past twenty-six years of teaching Chin Na, Judo and Chinese wrestling, I have instructed just about every type of person, privately or in mixed groups, old and young, men and women, boys and girls, sometimes all in the same class. I have learned to use the most direct, simple language backed with understandable examples to get my point across. Let me continue in that same vein here.

David Chow, master of Chin Na.

I normally begin my instruction to a group of new students by saying, "I am your chief instructor. I do not like any of you." I will pause, examine their facial responses, then add that "I do not dislike any of you either because I do not know you yet." I let this thought sink in for a moment, carefully watching the students as they begin to understand what I have said. I will then indicate to them that from my experience some thirty per cent, or three out of every ten students sitting there, will end up wasting their time, effort and money by giving up and dropping out of class after only a few weeks of training. They will quit because they did not follow my instructions properly in class or failed to practice at home. The early lessons may seem too strenuous for some because their bodies are not conditioned. Unfortunately, those in this group cannot be coerced into following the training advice. It is something you must want to do yourself. A martial art is not a game to play or something that is handed to you. It is an acquired discipline that becomes a strong character builder.

I will also lose students who become injured. Yes, there will be one out of ten, or ten per cent of the class, lost to injury. This small percentage will hurt themselves mainly because of an overeagerness to learn too much too fast without a solid foundation. Their ambitions will be way beyond their physical capabilities. They will strain or try too hard and even should an injury be avoided they will lose heart and quit because they did not achieve immediate mastery of the art. This is something like a horse running full speed during the first part of the race. He will usually end up last.

Nevertheless, six out of ten will stick with it, learn, and accomplish what I expect of them and achieve what they expect of themselves. A mutual respect will grow. The sixty per cent will be the future masters of the martial arts. I will tell the new class, "I can instruct and advise you but I cannot control or tell you who will be the dropouts and I do not know who will give it up because of an injury. I am leaving that up to you. From this moment on you must determine which group you want to belong to. I will give all of you the right to refuse to do what I instruct, but only if you do not understand the purpose of the particular training. However, once you do understand the significance, then I must expect you to perform wholeheartedly because it's for your own ultimate benefit."

My teaching is based on common sense. This basic intelligence is sometimes missed the first time around. For instance, the greater your achievement, the greater your personal reward. With Kung Fu meaning "total accomplishment," it is understood that anything worth achieving is usually difficult, requiring a lot of effort and stamina. Total concentration is mandatory for ultimate accomplishment. During the lessons, students are required to free their minds and empty their thoughts of outside desires. Their six senses should have one purpose—to learn what is being taught to them. I can remember when I was a teen-ager learning Kung Fu from my master Tung Tsung Nee. At the end of the lesson he would sometimes ask the class, "Who noticed that it had started to rain during class this evening?" Some of us raised our hands, having noticed a short while ago that it certainly was raining outside the training hall. Then he would respond in a soft-spoken voice, "Those who raised their hands and noticed the rain outside are those who are not totally concentrating on their training here inside. Since it does not involve your training, you should not have noticed the rain." There is no time for wandering thoughts or daydreaming during training hours.

I sometimes catch beginning students off guard by asking them, "Who are the three teachers here in the class?" They will all recognize me as the first teacher but become puzzled about the identity of the second and third instructors. I let them ponder the question for a moment, then inform them that their second teacher is their eyes. "You watch and you learn." The third teacher is your ears. "You listen and you learn." Therefore, if the student is merely physically in the class, not watching or listening, he is dismissing two vital teachers from himself. He deprives himself of his own natural teachers, and the third teacher, the class instructor, will not be heard or seen. This means that students in the presence of a Kung Fu master should have only one definite thought on their minds—learn what he is teaching. There should be no other reason for the students to be there. Think about that. Since students cannot teach each other how to master the art, they will have no business in carrying on conversations with each other during class time. To achieve pure concentration during a philosophical lecture or an explanation of movement, the student must attain the feeling that he is alone with only his master in the class, regardless of the number of students actually there. Absorb his philosophy. Learn his demonstrated techniques. I often tell my youngest students that, if any one of them lets his mind drift away, the observant instructor will have to stop the entire class, interrupt everyone's class time, effort and concentration, walk across the room and spank the inattentive youngster's bottom. This disciplinary measure is taken for only one reason, an unselfish one designed to wake him up and cause him to learn as much as the others are learning and to stimulate him to use his time wisely. The master must then return to the front of the class and resume the interrupted teaching. If your teacher shows this kind of concern for your individual learning, what should you say to him? You should say, "Thank you, Master."

Some of the common sense rules that I enforce in class include the keeping of finger and toenails trimmed short to prevent the scratching or hurting of another student. Students are required to wear clean uniforms or clothing in class. This means that other students will not be forced to smell disagreeable body odors at close contact. Students working out in street clothes must remove all articles from their pockets. Rattling coins might have a tendency to distract a fellow student's thoughts. In addition, time could be wasted looking for articles which might be dropped out of pockets. Students could also be scratched or hurt should they happen to land on a dropped key chain or other sharp object.

Now let's talk about the requirements of learning a Kung Fu art. To understand this point, let me use this illustration. Think of a solidly prepared soldier defending his country at the front line of a war zone. *First,* the fighting man must have a highly serviceable weapon, *second,* he must be physically fit to handle the weapon effectively, and, *third,* he should have a shield, or bulletproof vest, in case the enemy might shoot at him first. The soldier may be protected by the shield and survive. We can say that a Kung Fu art is like an effective weapon. However, merely having a potent weapon in your hand, knowing the theories of a Kung Fu art, will not ensure effective application. Without basic physical fitness, martial arts techniques may not be properly executed. Modern science is creating a tendency for mankind, in general, to withdraw from vigorous or rough-and-tumble physical endeavors. Twentieth-century man no longer has to chase for his food, hike for water, or climb for safety. This seems to indicate that mankind does not necessarily have to be physically strong to survive with most life support systems available at the push of a button. I, of course, cannot agree with this lazy way of life. In order to become a Kung Fu master today, as in ancient times, a sound body is required. Scheduled exercise is an essential part of training to maintain every part of the body. This is the only way to become a potential martial arts master. For example, if a student avoids leg exercises, he will never be able to deliver a strong and decisive kick to an opponent's vital point, or if he does not train his arms and hands, he will not be able to secure a solid lock on an aggressor's body.

I will compare the protective shield with the internal development of our bodies. We need an inner shield to avoid harm from a blow, a kick or a fall. Ch'i, a powerful internal safeguard when correctly cultivated, will be a major deterrent to injury. Strikes to the stomach, head, even the groin may be received without hurting the Kung Fu adept who throws up his protective shield of Ch'i. Chin Na, supported by Ch'i, has protective techniques of tumbling and breakfall, as it is called, to eliminate or minimize possible injuries should a practitioner be thrown or fall to the ground. I can compare this technique with a bowling ball. If you let the heavy ball drop out of your hand straight down to the floor, there will either be a flattened point on the ball or a dent in the floor because of the hard, direct impact. On the other hand, you can release the same ball with a circular swing of your arm. It will land in a rolling motion. The total weight of the ball will not be concentrated in one point. It will be distributed over the perimeter of the ball. Every inch of the perimeter will carry a portion of the entire weight of the rolling ball without damaging the floor or marring the ball. A falling human body may react with the same principle. Do not land with all your body weight on any one point such as an elbow, knee, shoulder or the head. Something will have to give, and it is a safe bet that it will not be the floor. Some part of the body will suffer. Muscles will be strained or bones will be broken. Instead, roll all your weight over through your arms, shoulders, back, hips and legs. As you hit the ground you can learn to roll from any angle so that every portion of your body will carry a small percentage of your own total weight, just like the bowling ball. You will learn to escape injury.

To repeat, learning only the forms or movements of a Kung Fu art is simply not enough. The student must be in excellent physical shape to complement and carry out the techniques. For his own safety, he must know how to receive and neutralize an offensive force.

All students should have a clearly defined understanding of Kung Fu training. The following are the seven requirements for becoming a proficient practitioner of a martial art:

1. **Have faith in your selected style of martial arts.** Without a steadfast belief in your system, interest will diminish and mastery will not be achieved.

2. **Respect your chosen Master,** who has sincerely accepted you as his student. Recognize his knowledge and ability as being most worthy of emulation.

3. **Concentrate during training.** A strong discipline will result along with a more rapid mastery of the art. A close mental concentration will intensify physical strength.

4. **Cultivate patience during training.** Your goal will be reached in good time with proper application. A calm endurance and self-possession will also aid in the resistance of any potential provocation.

5. **Practice co-ordination during training.** The ability to move with a harmonious and instantaneous adjustment to any situation will provide a more immediate mastery of the art.

6. **Practice as much as possible** not only in the training hall but at home. Every hour of practice will deepen and solidify your basic foundation to prepare for a higher level of training. Consistent practical performance or application of knowledge leads to certain proficiency.

7. **Acquire confidence in yourself through your art.** This state of mind implies a cool self-reliance under any circumstances. It offers the assurance of poise and imperturbability in the face of any danger.

Since the start of the "Kung Fu" television series, literally thousands of letters have come to my attention as the show's technical director. The most common questions were "Which martial art is better?" and "What system of Kung Fu is more effective?" Well, to me, these are improper questions. It would be as if I were to ask, "What is more important—air, water or earth?" They are all important. They are all vital. If you are drowning, the earth could be your lifesaver. If you are suffocating, you must have oxygen. If you are lost in the desert and dying of thirst, then a pool of fresh water would save your life. You may draw upon these three elements, air, water and earth, for self-preservation. They are the necessities of life. In the same way you may draw upon any Chinese martial art for self-preservation and survivorship. Any recognized self-defense system will benefit physical fitness, co-ordination, patience, concentration and confidence. All of the Chinese systems seek the same goal. Some merely approach it from a different path. When any true martial artist practices hard or soft movements, say, in front of a mirror, he will have only one thought in his mind—the efficient application of the technique in order to survive an attack or to protect others from intruding violence. Every practiced strike, block, or kick, every maneuver of the body should be concentrated and focused just as if it were a real combat situation. With the total effort in mind and after several years of training not only will you master your Kung Fu art but you will master yourself as a person. You will have achieved most assuredly good health and longevity. I must mention that there are those, however, who have killing on their minds during training. A militant character or a fierce appearance may be developed over the years. This is why premeditated aggression is never taught or condoned by a legitimate Chinese master. Wanton violence and killing are against every law in martial arts and against every law in nature. As humans, we are the only beings who kill needlessly. We are the only beings on earth who destroy things merely on a whim or capricious notion. The rest of the animal world will only kill for food or protection. Chinese martial arts training is geared to the philosophy of nature's way. A student should never think of killing during practice. Instead, he should think that he is saving himself from harm or a helpless baby from a mad dog. In the case of an actual conflict situation that is absolutely unavoidable but is justifiable for you to intervene and execute the necessary self-defense techniques to survive or protect, then the following principles should be clearly remembered and acted upon:

Determination.

A hidden strength resides in all of us. This supernormal power may be brought out but only through the exercise of a firm resolve which is supported by the flow of Ch'i and adrenaline. In the midst of violence, a martial arts master will show total determination against an attack. Exuding a quality of invincibility, the master simply knows, through his own resoluteness, that he will decide or determine the outcome of the aggression. He realizes that any laxness or undetermined actions will only create advantages for the opponent. Therefore, he must use not only his physical ability but his willpower or perseverance of the mind to subdue an attack.

Calmness.

Common sense tells us that mental turmoil or internal agitation will reduce co-ordination, slow down reflexes and throw off accuracy. An unruffled mind is necessary for the efficient application of techniques. As in the tranquil eye of a hurricane, the master's mind remains cool, composed and collected in the face of violence. This mental quality of unclouded tranquillity while defending against vicious aggression takes great dedication to master. It is well worth the time and effort to attain complete composure for the mind. The conquest of mental agitation will lead to the conquest of outside disturbance.

Conservation and calculation of movement.

Human energy, after repeated transmissions of power, begins to diminish and eventually becomes ineffective. All force has its final moment. It is like an arrow released into the sky; when its strength is exhausted, it turns and falls to the ground, deadened, unable to move. It is the same with human beings. Spent energy or loss of strength means that a weakness has been created. That weakness could prove fatal. Without a fully capable or fresh defense, there will always be a greater susceptibility to attack. Since every action takes time and effort, a master will try to maintain optimum agility and endurance by avoiding any unnecessary movements. By conserving energy, he will be more able to keep his body in a safe and sound condition for a longer period of time. Instantly calculated and decisive response to aggression which produces the maximum effect with a minimum effort will come only after a long practice and experience.

Power through balance.

Total and effective power may only be delivered through a balanced body. The reality of this statement may be tested in many ways. For example, if a student wears only one big-heeled boot and his other foot is bare, let him try to lift a heavy object. He will find it will be easier if he wears two boots or none at all. A student may try to deliver a punch by standing on tiptoes with just one foot. A maximum power blow will be impossible to execute from that precarious position. Balance is vital for effective performance. The master's goal is to retain his balance at all times while breaking or disrupting his opponent's steadiness and equilibrium. There will be room for only one balanced body in the close body contact art of Chin Na. When a master maintains his balance during a perfectly executed technique, then the opponent obviously will suffer an imbalance. On the other hand, if the master loses his balance, his opponent will solidify his own balance and win the match through the master's unbalanced position. Imbalance leads to submission. This is why the practice of continuous balance is so vital. It is the essential ingredient of Chin Na. Other martial artists tend to agree on this point, saying that balance is the most important part of any self-defense.

On a personal note, the first time I ever saw my grand master Tung Tsung Nee in Shanghai, he was just getting on his bicycle. The reason that I happened to look over was that he did not get on the usual way of simply swinging one leg over the bicycle. Instead, while the bike was at a standstill, he grasped both handlebars and, using only his hands and arms, raised his body onto the vehicle. I mean that he did not swing or throw himself up onto the bicycle; he used only his arm power to lift himself onto the motionless two-wheeler. He then rode off leaving an astonished bystander, me, wondering how he did it. As a young boy, I was impressed with that casual display of acrobatic balance and power, and I began to think that there was a lot to learn from this stately gentleman. Later when I enrolled in Grand Master Tung's class, during my very first lesson he asked me to approach the front of the class. I did as he asked. With some thirty other students watching, he asked me, "Young Tai Wai [Tai Wai is the

攻心為上
攻城為次
攻人為下

佟忠義

Favorite philosophy of Grand Master Tung Tsung Nee:
Winning the hearts is the best way.
Winning the castles is the secondary way.
Winning through domination is the worst way.

Mandarin word for "David"], do you know how to stand?" I replied, "Yes, I think I do." Then, as he stood directly in front of me, he performed a sudden leg sweep that sent both of my legs straight up in the air while my head was going straight down. Grand Master Tung gently caught my neck and cradled it in his palm, protecting my head from hitting the concrete. (He maintained a rigorous training program with outdoor practice on a concrete floor covered with one thin rug.) Grand Master Tung told me, "There is no man who can balance himself in all directions at the same time, unless he has six legs. In the event that somehow you lose your supporting balance and fall you have to learn how to break the fall and avoid landing on a vital point." Thus, my first lesson in Chin Na was a warning about keeping my balance and knowing how to protect myself if I ever lost it. Grand Master Tung made me realize that balance is not only the key to standing, it is the key to life.

Direct approach.

The quickest approach to gain control with the least effort comes from the shortest and most direct route. This is accomplished by keeping the arms and legs as near as possible to the central balance point. Overextended limbs result in a loss of efficient body power. Whether the first move is defensive or offensive, the body should be positioned close to the opponent to permit the second move to be shorter and more direct. The first technique also could lead the opponent himself to move closer so the master may follow with a more compact movement. This Chin Na concept of directness may be summed up by paraphrasing the old American expression of "getting there firstest with the mostest by using the leastest."

Pain and pressure flows.

The application of pressure to certain parts of the body creates pain, which will cause the antagonist to curtail his aggression. By twisting certain joints or pressing selected nerve points, pain impulses are immediately picked up by strained or sprained nerve endings which travel instantaneously through other free nerve endings or so-called pain receptors to the brain, where it is computer-processed into the sensation of pain. Pain is always a symptom that something has gone wrong with the opponent's plan. With the application of a Chin Na technique, the attacker would be advised to yield or the pain could be intensified by increased pressure. Pain means that a warning signal is being sent out to stop something or begin beneficial corrective measures. From this point of view, pain can be considered to be a lifesaver or, at the very least, a blessing to prevent broken bones, displaced joints or torn ligaments. However, pain must be sufficiently severe to force the adversary to accept its warning. Properly applied pressure to one part of the body will have the effect of demobilizing the entire physical system. For example, if the practitioner has a total lock, backed by intense pressure, on the opponent's left arm, he will not have to worry about the knife the aggressor holds in his right hand.

This might sound like a bold statement, but it can be and has been tested in practice and in the streets. In seeking immediate relief from suffering, the combatant often will react with fear and anxiety. He will see the distinct possibility that the situation might get worse now that he has no control over what is happening. He will have no recourse except to give up his attack or suffer indefinite pain or debilitation to his body. However, in rare cases when the assailant is mentally deranged, pain may not always affect his wild actions. The master should withdraw or escape a confrontation such as this. Should the violent mental case not permit this, the Chin Na expert would be forced to offer a conclusive technique to the unfortunate individual after all other restraining methods failed.

BASIC TECHNIQUES OF CHIN NA

The following movements and tactics are presented as examples of basic Chin Na techniques. Every Chin Na student must learn the following moves with his master. Since we do not believe that a reader can master any martial art by simply absorbing material from a printed page or book, we offer these illustrations to give a firm idea of what Chin Na movements look like and how they are applied. We emphasize that many of these movements should be practiced under the supervision of a recognized Chin Na master. Improperly applied pressure or locks can be fatal. It has happened with inexperienced and irresponsible individuals. With that advisory, read on.

1

2   2A

3   3A

4   4A

5

6

LESSON ONE

DEFENSE
AGAINST SINGLE HAND
WRIST GRABBING

(Left Hand Grabs Left Hand)

We shall remember that nobody's hand is big enough to wrap around your wrist twice. Therefore, when an attacker grabs your wrist, there shall always be a gap. That break-through point is between the attacker's thumb and four fingers (photo 2A). When suddenly grabbed, always attempt to maneuver your body to maintain your balance. Do not forcefully resist the aggressor's initial pushing or pulling. Go with his motion; otherwise he will just push or pull you that much harder. Calculate the right timing to make your escape move. Tighten your fist and twist your wrist so that the narrow part of your wrist is pointing toward the gap of the attacker's grabbing hand (photo 3A). With a sharp outward motion you may easily slip your wrist from his grasp. When your left hand is free, your right elbow should be no more than a foot away from his jaw (photo 4A). Using powerful hip action extended through your right shoulder into your right elbow, strike the antagonist in the jaw with your elbow (photo 5). He should withdraw from further contention.

DEFENSE AGAINST SINGLE HAND WRIST GRABBING

(Left Hand Grabs Right Hand)

The theory of Lesson One will apply to this second lesson. When an attacker grabs your right wrist, whether he pulls or pushes you, you should not resist him with your full strength, as already mentioned in Lesson One. Close your fist and turn your wrist (photo 3). Pry your wrist from the opponent's hand through the gap in his grip (photo 4). At the same time, his resistance will throw his body slightly forward. In his forward motion (photos 5 and 6), you should respond instantly by giving him a right hand back-fist punch to his face (photos 7, 8 and 9), smashing the nose, which will create immediate pain and his retreat.

7

8

9

LESSON THREE

DEFENSE
AGAINST SINGLE HAND
WRIST GRABBING

(Right Hand Grabs Right Hand)

When an assailant grabs your right wrist with his right hand (photo 2A), respond by grasping his right hand with your free left hand (photo 3A). Then maneuver the fingers of your detained right hand over the top of his right wrist (photo 4A). Grasp tightly. Shuffle your body a half step toward the combatant as both of your hands start to apply a twisting pressure lock to his right hand. This action occurs while you are pulling in your arms close to your chest (photo 4). Then, using the bottom edge of your right hand, rapidly apply hard pressure to his attacking hand. The attacker will be obliged to bend forward, helplessly reeling from the intense pain in his wrist (photos 5 and 5A). A left foot kick to the head (photo 6) will be most effective in concluding the uninvited intrusion.

6

7

8

1

2

2A

3

4

4A

5

5A

6

6A

LESSON FOUR

DEFENSE
AGAINST SINGLE HAND
WRIST GRABBING

(Right Hand Against Left)

The principles of Lesson Three will also apply to this lesson (photos 2 and 2A). First, using your free right hand, get a firm hold on the assaulting hand (photo 4A). Then raise your left elbow and turn your body into his arm as you apply heavy pressure to the attacker's wrist (photos 5 and 5A). Do not lean forward to impose pressure. Instead, you should turn your shoulders so that the left shoulder and elbow go down and the right shoulder goes up (photo 6A). This move ensures that your body will be totally balanced while the opponent's body will remain painfully restrained (photo 6).

LESSON FIVE

DEFENSE
AGAINST SINGLE HAND
WRIST GRABBING

(Right Hand
Against Right Hand from Inside)

When an offender seizes your wrist from the inside (photo 2A), you can see that your fingers are still free. Even though your wrist is being held, you can use the unrestrained fingers to grab his attacking wrist as you draw back your free left arm (photos 3 and 3A). Maintaining your balance, pull his attacking hand past your body as you maneuver yourself behind him. Push your chest forward. This move will lock his elbow across your chest. At the same time, slam your free left forearm across his head or neck (photos 4 and 4A and feature photo at left). As you straighten your body and push out your chest, the attacker begins to lose his balance. These three movements, right arm back, chest out, and left arm out, should be done simultaneously in a sharp motion. Then drive your knee into the middle of his back while snapping his body backward (photo 5). With the opponent landing on his back (photo 6), hang onto his right hand and deliver a crushing knee-drop blow to his chest (photo 7). Further submission strikes may be applied if necessary.

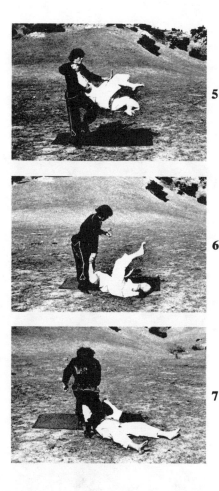

DOUBLE WRIST GRABBING DEFENSE

(Upward Wrist Grabbing)

When an attacker faces you and upwardly grabs both (or one) of your wrists (photo 2), do not struggle or strain violently against him or he will grab you tighter and push you harder. Instead, in a single concentrated effort, make one sharp downward strike with both arms. Slam the lower edge of your wrist straight down against the opponent's thumbs. To avoid hitting your own thighs, however, always spread your arms as wide as your shoulders as you strike downward against his thumbs. Not only will he then lose his grip but your momentum will carry him toward the ground (photos 3, 3A and 4). With the aggressor positioned lower than you are, it will not be totally effective to punch downward at close range with your fist. In this case it will be simpler to smash your right elbow into his jaw (photo 5). Supported by the directed power of your hip and shoulder and braced by your left arm, the powerful impact of your right elbow can easily break the antagonist's jaw.

1

2

3

2A

3A

4

5

6

DOUBLE WRIST GRABBING DEFENSE

(Downward Wrist Grabbing)

An antagonist might seize one of your wrists with both of his hands (photo 2). Respond by using your free left hand to reach over and through the attacker's arms (photo 3). Grab your own detained fist and pull straight up between his thumbs (photos 4 and 5). Follow up with a direct backhand fist to the groin (photos 6, 6A and 7), a most effective conclusion to the aggression.

7

8

8A

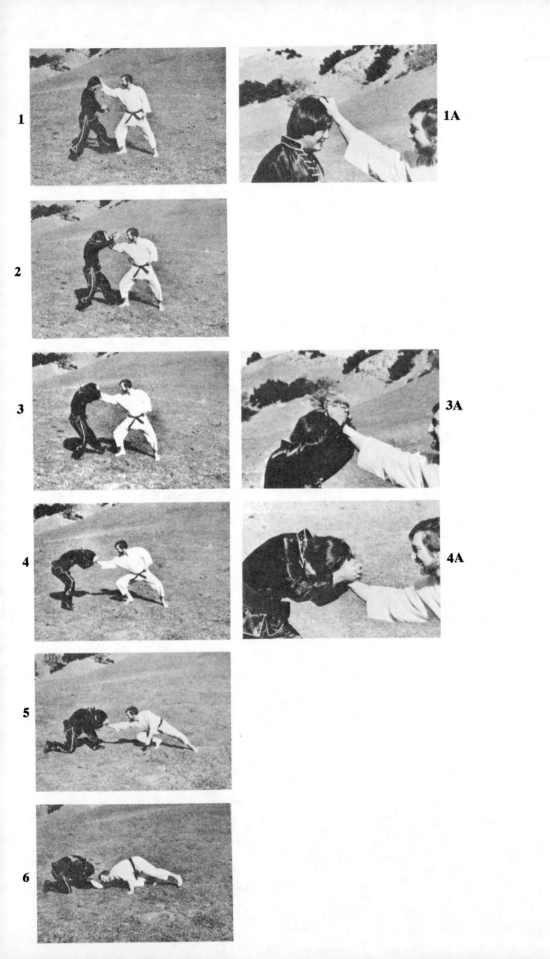

1

1A

2

3

3A

4

4A

5

6

LESSON EIGHT

DEFENSE AGAINST HAIR GRABBING

Should someone assault you by grabbing your hair, he will be most probably yanking, pulling or pushing it (photo 1). Since your hair is connected to your head and your head controls your balance, you must react instantaneously to avoid losing your body control by putting both of your hands on the back of his seizing right hand next to his wrist (photos 3 and 3A). This means that he is no longer just holding onto your hair. In effect, he is yanking at your total body weight, which is difficult for one hand, especially at this angle. Examine closely photos 4, 5 and 6. Notice that as you hang onto his hair-grabbing hand, you should drop to one knee while moving slightly backward to throw him off balance. In the same move, bend your wrist and neck to about forty-five degrees downward. With his right hand locked in by both of your hands against your head, that angle is important. The sudden downward pressure of your full body weight will cause his right hand to be forced backward against his wrist joint. He will have no choice but to follow you toward the ground. If he does not release his grip by then, his wrist will be broken.

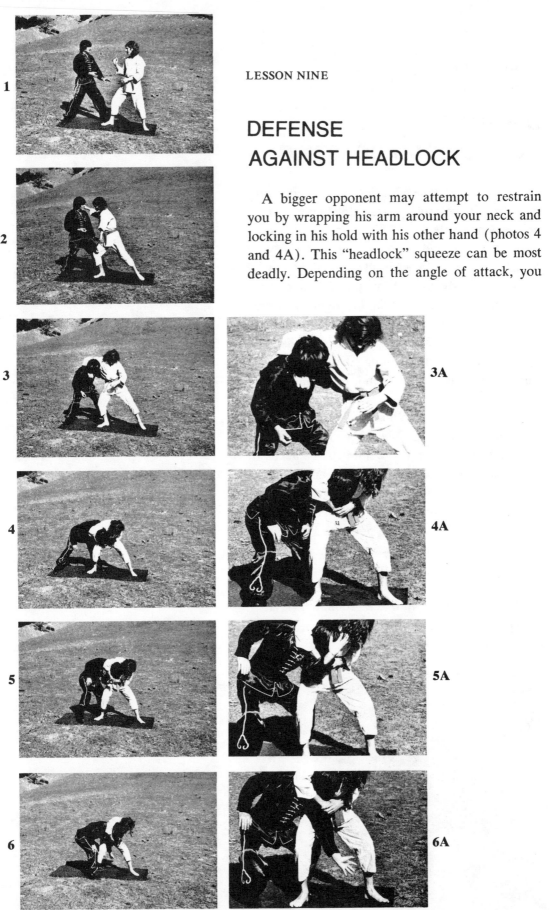

1

2

DEFENSE
AGAINST HEADLOCK

A bigger opponent may attempt to restrain you by wrapping his arm around your neck and locking in his hold with his other hand (photos 4 and 4A). This "headlock" squeeze can be most deadly. Depending on the angle of attack, you

3   3A

4   4A

5   5A

6   6A

could be strangled or your neck broken. Therefore, you must respond instantly to regain your balance by taking a full step forward with your right foot. Place it in front of the attacker's right foot (photo 6). At the same time, place your left knee behind his right knee and slide your left hand out in front of you (photo 6A). Use your left hand to grab behind his left knee (photo 7A). His left leg will then be blocked by your left hand and his right leg blocked by your left knee. Use your shoulder to bump him over backward while simultaneously using your left arm to pull his left leg forward. Losing his balance, he will be turned upside down (as shown in the feature photo below). The defense against the headlock has more intricate moves than in the previous lessons. So follow each step carefully in slow motion with your partner. You will gain speed as you become more familiar with each movement.

7

7A

DEFENSE AGAINST LAPEL GRABBING

If a belligerent individual, using his right hand, grabs the lapels of your jacket or clothing in front of your chest (photo 2A), use your right hand to seize his offending hand. Put your palm over the top of his hand and wrap your fingers as far as possible under his palm. Press his hand tightly against your chest (photos 3A and 4A) as you twist your body to the right and bow forward. The attacker's elbow will turn upward, permitting you to strike his elbow with your forearm (photos 4, 5, 5A and the feature photo below). He will then drop low because of the pressure and pain. End his belligerence with a right foot kick to his face (photos 7 and 8).

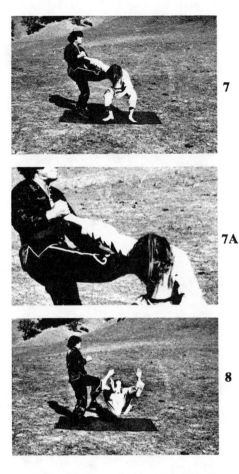

7

7A

8

DEFENSE AGAINST LUNGING THRUST PUNCH

Should you see an assailant lunging toward you, preparing to deliver a straight thrust punch with his right hand, do not try to avoid his knockout attempt by suddenly retreating. His forward momentum will be faster than you could ever move backward. So stand your ground and dodge his big punch to the head by diverting the direction of his oncoming fist. This can be done simply by moving your head to the left side and using your left hand, sharply batting his fist to your right. When he unexpectedly misses your jaw, his momentum will carry him forward and off balance. Your right palm should be waiting for him in a well-balanced position (photo 3). As he runs into you, jab the bottom part of your palm below his nose, under his chin or into his throat (photo 4). With his force driving in and yours speeding out (photos 5, 6, 7 and 8) the attacker's self-motivated predicament could be likened to his running in the dark and being caught under the chin by a clothes wire (see feature photo).

7

8

1

2

2A

3

4

5

6

LESSON TWELVE

DEFENSE
AGAINST LEFT JAB

A left jab is a popular punch in any boxer's arsenal. It is as essential to learn how to evade a jab as it is whistling toward your head. Pivot your head, body and hip sharply to the right so that you begin to face the same general direction he faces as he pokes the jab at you (photos 1 and 2). Hook your left wrist under his left wrist; simultaneously, strike his left elbow with your right palm (photo 2A). Remember—dodging your head, twisting your hips, hooking his wrist and smashing his elbow—all these movements are to be done in a flowing, split-second motion. While your attacker worries about his injured elbow, you then should grab either his hair or collar with your right hand and pull backward. In the same motion, use your right foot to sweep up his left foot (photo 5). After he lands on the ground, disable the aggressor with a hammer-fist punch to the stomach or groin, or a chop to the neck (photos 7, 8 and feature photo below).

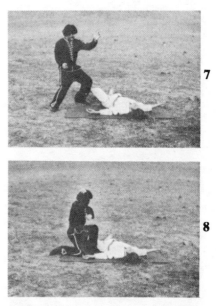

7

8

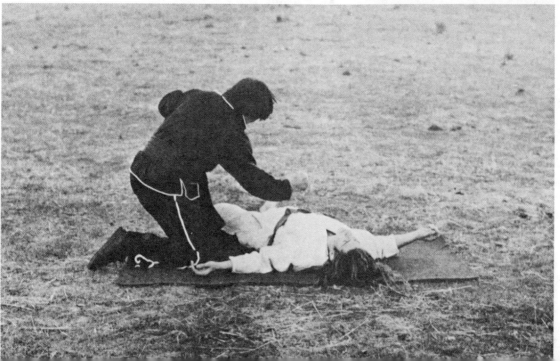

1

2

3

4

5

6

DEFENSE AGAINST A KICK

Kicks to the body or to the head are always dangerous. The best way to avoid their maximum impact is to sidestep or pivot away from the pounding-in foot, and counter by hooking an arm, the left one in this example, under the kicking leg and grabbing around the knee (photos 2 and 3). He will then have only one foot planted on the ground as you lift up his other leg (photo 4). Drive in your own right leg and hook it around his left leg (photo 5), while your right hand smashes against his chest. Down he goes (photo 6). With your left arm still hanging onto his right leg, he will be in a perfect position for a knee to the groin (photos 7 and 8). His kicks will not be so powerful after that devastating strike.

7

8

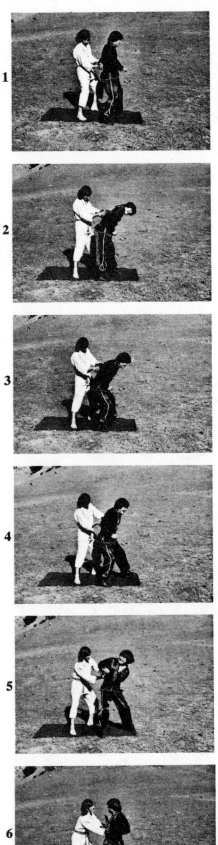

1

2

3

4

5

6

1A

DEFENSE AGAINST SINGLE ARM TWIST

The arm twist to the back is one of the oldest restraining techniques known to man. It is simple, effective and painful. Therefore, you must know how to get out of this hold. Should your left arm be wrenched upward behind your back (photos 1 and 2), never try to escape by turning your body to the left. This move will only increase the pressure-pain and cause potential damage to the nerves, tendons, muscles and bones in the left shoulder. Instead, take a strong left step forward (photo 4) and snap your hips to the right so that you almost fully face the attacker (photos 5 and 6). If he continues to hold onto your wrist, then his body will be forced forward and slightly downward. As shown in photos

6A

7

8

6 and 6A, your right arm should swing around while cocked in tight to your body. Your right palm then should be triggered like a bullet to hit below his nose, under his chin or into his throat (photos 7 and 8). On the other hand, reader, should your right arm be twisted up behind your back, reverse the procedure and take a right step forward, turn to the left and continue the above technique. You should always practice the arm twist defense with both arms. You never know which arm might be wrested up around your back.

LESSON FIFTEEN

DEFENSE AGAINST FORWARD NECK CHOKE

Anyone who violently chokes you is usually not fooling around. He could easily choke you to death if you did not respond properly. Should a powerful attacker face you and squeeze both hands around your neck with his thumbs jamming into your throat, obviously the main thing to do is immediately disengage the stranglehold because the ordinary throat cannot resist an extremely strong choke for more than a few seconds without caving in. (Throat-muscle tensing also can be used, but we will not go into that here.) First, clasp your hands tightly together (photos 2 and 2A). Keep both elbows in together as close as possible. Then ram both fists up between the assailant's arms (photos 3 and 3A). This sharp move will not only release his two-handed grip, but will bring your own arms above his head. Smash his head downward with your hands as you crash your knee up into his face (photos 4 and 5). This head-on collision should be enough to stop his choking-death attack. As the feature photo at right indicates, the ill-disposed combatant is left open for some deadly follow-up kicks or stomps.

1

2

2A

3

3A

4

4A

5

DEFENSE
AGAINST
CHOKE FROM BACK

When surprised by a sudden choking attack from the rear, you should immediately squat down into a strong horse stance to regain your balance (photo 3). Reach behind you and grab both opposing hands; circle your head under his arms, causing his choke hold to be broken (photos 4 and 5). As you finish the circle, still controlling his arms (photo 6), which are helplessly crossed left over right, continue the twisting motion against his arms (photo 7). Turn both of his hands counterclockwise until the elbows lock together at the breaking point (photo 8). Aided by a snap kick to the groin or left leg (again photo 8), he will flip over on his back (photo 9). Then should he try to get up and continue his fight, you may deliver a discouraging head stomp.

SINGLE ARM
NECK CHOKE FROM REAR

When someone chokes you from behind with a single arm, he usually wants to throw you off balance by pulling you backward, as well as cutting off your oxygen supply. Respond by dropping your body (photo 3) to regain your balance. Then, braced by your left hand, raise your right elbow (photo 4) and slam it into his rib cage (photo 5). If he still does not let you go, grab his right arm or sleeve, swing your hip into his lower midsection (photo 6) and give him an old-fashion hip throw, since he is positioned for that move anyway (photo 7 and feature photo at right). As he hits the ground (photo 8), follow up with a knee-drop to the same area where you elbowed him. To attack an already injured spot will hasten an end to the conflict.

7

8

9

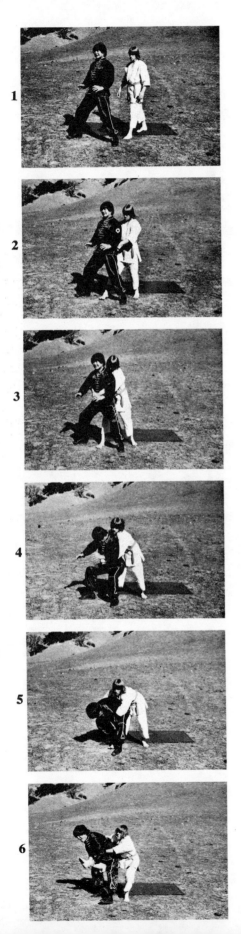

1

2

3

4

5

6

DEFENSE AGAINST WAIST GRABBING FROM BEHIND

Never swing to the right and left after an assailant grabs and squeezes your waist from behind. You will not be able to get out of his grip that way. He will only be inclined to tighten his hold. Instead, you should sink your weight and drop your body as quickly and heavily as possible (photo 4). Feeling your hip touching one of his knees, instantly bend down and seize his right ankle with both hands (photo 5). As you pull it up between your legs (photo 6), simply sit down on his right knee. The pressure against the bone and knee joint will force him to the ground (photo 7). Retain a firm grip on his ankle and swing your right leg and body around to the right (photo 8). Your turning will cause his ankle to turn. The rest of his body will follow or else something in his leg will have to give or snap (photo 9). Then use your heel to stomp on his kidney. This technique is especially useful for youngsters and females.

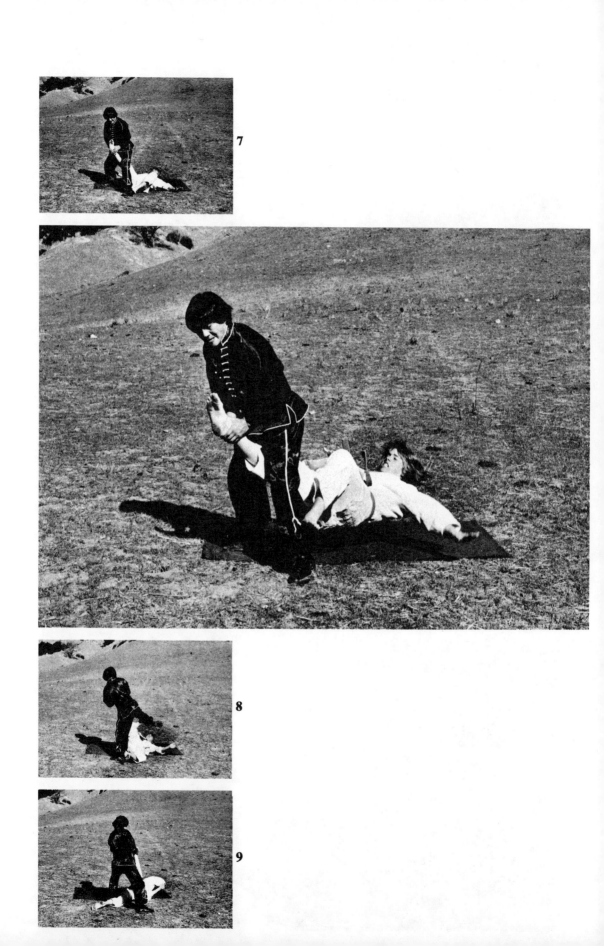

7

8

9

LESSON NINETEEN

DEFENSE AGAINST BEAR HUG WITH VICTIM'S ARMS FREE

A normal person will last only about a minute or so if some big brute applies a crushing bear hug to the midsection. A bear hug from the front (or back) can knock your wind out or, more seriously, injure or break your spine or rib cage. When caught off guard, you will need both legs on the ground to maintain a minimum balance. In this example, your arms are free, as are your

legs. Remember that you should always use your free parts to attack the weakest part of the aggressor's body. In this case, place your left hand on the back of his head and your right palm under his chin with your fingers facing outward (photos 2, 3 and 3A). This gives you a firm grip on his head. Then snap his head around in a sharp counterclockwise movement (photo 4). Unnerved by the sudden, unexpected twisting jolt in his neck, he will release his bear hug (photos 5 and 5A). This technique is based on the principle that any average person's arms can summon enough strength to twist a strong man's neck, especially if done by surprise. To decisively conclude the encounter, you can very conveniently raise your knee up into his groin (photo 7).

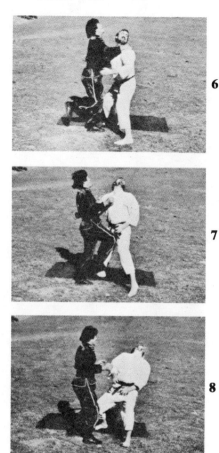

6

7

8

DEFENSE AGAINST BEAR HUG WITH VICTIM'S ARMS LOCKED

You will experience a feeling of anxiety, if not outright fear, should you ever be grabbed in an unexpected bear hug with your arms locked in, especially if your body is arched backward (photo 3). You will not be able to use your arms, legs or knees with any efficiency. If the attacker is big enough, he literally might pick you up and carry you away. But, in an effort to lessen alarm, remember that there is one vital part of your body that remains free and movable. That is your head. Attract his attention and make him look at you for just a fraction of a second, plenty of time for you to bang your forehead against the bridge of his nose (photos 4, 4A and feature photo below). This should release the bear hug for sure, since a hit to the nose will cause instant pain (photos 5 and 5A). Then drop to your knees and pound a straight punch into his solar plexus (photos 6 and 7). As your antagonist doubles up, reach down and pull his trousers forward (photo 8). He will fall on his back (photo 9). With his legs spread open facing you (photo 10), a most opportune disabling strike would be a downward thrust punch to the groin (photos 11 and 12). He will not "bear hug," or even plain hug, anyone for a while after that experience.

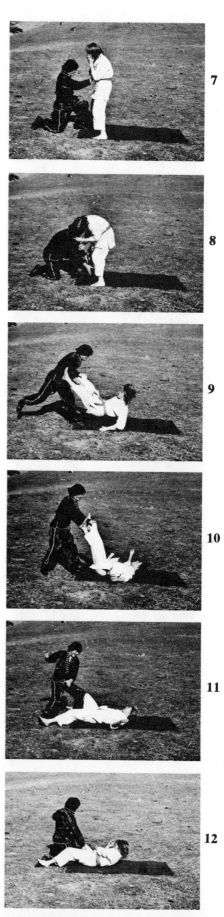

7

8

9

10

11

12

1

2

2A

3

4

4A

5

5A

6

DEFENSE AGAINST OVERHEAD KNIFE ATTACK

A knife can be a most lethal extension of the hand. But despite its deadly possibilities a knife-wielding assailant can be handled and disarmed. Should you face an attacker lunging at you while raising a knife to stab you, do not try to back-peddle or jump backward. As previously mentioned, he can always run forward faster than you can run backward. You should, instead, stand your ground and stop the knife just as he raises his hand against you; ideally, even before he has a chance to exert a full-power downward stroke toward your body. This is done by making a kind of fork with both of your hands against his right wrist (photos 2 and 2A) to hold back any downward thrust of the knife. Then, with your right leg, step in behind his right leg (photos 3 and 4). Grab his right wrist with your left hand as you bring your right hand under his armpit, up and over to cover your own right hand (photo 4A). You can see that this move provides a perfect armlock. Any sharp downward pressure should cause him to drop his blade (photos 5 and 5A). For insurance you may follow with an outer sweep throw (photo 6) by thrusting your right leg behind his right leg and pulling his locked right arm downward. End the actions of the would-be killer with strikes to the kidney or spine (photos 7 and 8).

1

2

3   3A

4

5  5A

6   6A

DEFENSE
AGAINST
UNDERHAND KNIFE ATTACK

When you see a knife aimed at your stomach from a low angle, do not stand and wait for the assailant to drive the blade in with his full force. You should defend by being the aggressor in this case. Jump in against his attacking knife hand before he has a chance to stab at you with total power (photos 2 and 3). Lock your elbows and form a fork with your hands (photo 3A) and stop the advance of the knife thrust. Then, while gripping his right hand with your left hand, spin into his attacking arm and chest (photos 4 and 5) and execute a crossed armlock to his right elbow (examine closely photo 5A). Bring your right arm under his right elbow, securing your right hand against your left forearm. During this instantaneous movement your back should feel his chest as you apply breaking pressure to his elbow, forcing him to drop the knife (photos 6 and 6A). If you then lean your entire body forward with his locked right arm, he will have to stand on his toes. Continue this forward motion with a right leg sweep, which will send his feet straight up in the air (feature photo below) with his head and back headed for the ground. The impact alone should make the attacker forget his evil intentions.

1

2

3

4

5

DEFENSE
AGAINST TWO-SIDE ATTACK

If two strong-arm types, one on each side of you, seize your arms and you know that their total combined strength is greater than yours, your response must be swift, direct and effective. As we again emphasize, do not struggle wildly to get loose, they will merely hold you tighter. What you should always do is plan ahead. When you make a feint in raising up your arms (photo 2), the attackers will normally react by pulling your arms back down. Herein lies the plan. At that split second use their own downward strength, now added to yours, to smash your fists down into their groins (photos 3 and 4). While they are doubled over in instant pain, balance yourself and drop down on your right knee (photo 5). Grab and yank their inside pant cuffs straight up (photos 6 and 7). They will go flying backward. This technique can also be used when there is only one arm-grabbing attacker at your side.

6

7

6.

The Dynamics of Kung

Chinese Pugilism and Kung

Kung, which can be interpreted as a highly focused and potent concentration of effort, is the mental foundation behind all hand and leg techniques in Chinese self-defense. The intensification of mind growth must be emphasized if you ever hope to truly master your selected style of Kung Fu. Your physical skill may appear excellent, even spectacular, but without Kung, supreme mastery is impossible.

For example, the fist is always stronger when aided by Kung. Kung is expressed through the fist, which, as Chinese masters claimed, if totally cultivated, made the practitioner so invincible that "not even a single hair could be damaged by the sharp edge of an attacker's sword."

Chinese martial artists of the past practiced two types of Kung: Internal and External. The Internal stresses Ch'i, meditate to be passive, while the External accentuates strength, which flows through the body without obstruction.

External methods were developed into two parts, Soft and Hard Kung. While the soft style is more difficult to perfect, there is no unusual appearance in a master of this Kung. He looks like an ordinary person, sometimes even shorter or more frail appearing than average. But should he be attacked, he invariably avoids harm's way. The Soft Kung master's defense is impenetrable, with no obvious physical tension or strain; it is as if the distance between him and the adversary is "tens of feet." The assailant, however, is subdued sharply, sometimes killed, even though the Soft Kung master never touches his body. This kind of Internal or mental Kung force can be absolutely terrifying; as a result it is also known as the Yin, or Negative, Kung. In feudal China, many martial artists felt that Yin Kung utilized unethical fighting techniques, i.e., those which caused harm to virtues, thus very few practiced this "undetectable art."

On the other hand, Hard Kung is manifested entirely on the outside, and is detectable. Muscle will bulge, nerves will strain and calluses will be formed. While this system is easier than Soft Kung training, the effects are similar, but the methods are different. A Hard Kung master, even if attacked with weapons, with a rapid concentration of strength, will be able to strike instantaneously, breaking the opponent's weapons. And when bearing a rock weighing several hundred pounds on his body and having the boulder struck with a sledge hammer, his body still remains intact while the rock is broken into pieces. However, this level of Hard Kung takes "tens of years" to achieve. Essentially, Hard Kung uses the strength of positive energy and is also known as Yang Kung. Since Hard Kung is easier to accomplish than the negative Soft Kung, most martial artists practice this Positive Kung. For instance, as will be explained, Iron Forearm and Horse Saddle Kung are Hard Kung, and Red Sand Palm and One Finger Kung are examples of rarely mastered forms of Soft Kung. But by knowing at least one form of a Positive Kung, according to venerable Chinese masters, "the body is strong and healthy, no knife or sword can cause harm, no illness can overpower, and no coldness or heat can hurt." Kung, combined with fist and leg techniques, ensures success. Each displays its own merits in unison yet fails in separation. There is a saying that "many Chinese practiced boxing but ignored Kung, so they were unsuccessful even in advanced years." This means that Kung training is mandatory, if not primary, for authentic martial arts accomplishment. But empty talk of Kung mastery will never produce the wished-for ability. We again emphasize that, to be successful, a would-be martial artist must practice regularly with firm resolve. Action produces results. Idleness produces nothing.

Patience is another key word. A would-be student, hearing of the benefits, cannot simply walk into a kwoon (training hall), spend a few weeks or months with a sifu (master) and walk out as an expert of a specialized Kung form. A lot of time is involved in actual training, perhaps many years. It is a serious investment of years in one's life. The attitude of calm endurance and self-possession must be acquired to eventually reap the benefits. Persist in what has been begun. He who commands patience may command what he wills. Talent grows strong through personal force; character becomes firm through the will.

Ancient Steps in Practicing Kung

The student must prepare himself for five restrictions:
1. He must not be frivolous.
2. He must not be conceited.
3. He must not be impatient.
4. He must not be negligent.
5. He must not be lascivious.

There are also seven detriments:
1. Fornication depletes the energy.
2. Anger harms the breathing.
3. Worry numbs the mind.
4. Overtrustfulness hurts the heart.
5. Overdrinking (of alcoholic beverage) dilutes the blood.
6. Laziness softens the muscles.
7. Tenseness weakens the bones.

Only by understanding the five restrictions and seven detriments can we start discussing the actual Kung practice of ancient times in China. They are all based on common sense application. For example, if someone constantly avoids exercise, obviously his muscles will remain soft and weak. So there is no time for laziness if strength is the student's goal. Without discipline, laziness will control his life. Initial Kung training is divided into several phases:

1. Stimulate the skin and muscles.
2. Exercise the tendons.
3. Exercise the power of the body joints.
4. Begin Ch'i development.

What is meant by exercising the skin and muscles? This means rubbing various parts of the body until the skin and muscles feel hot and appear red. For example, use both palms to briskly massage the calves. But palm rubbing must be done consistently. It must become a daily habit. If one is busy, for instance, during the day, the exercise can be performed regularly after getting up in the morning and before going to bed at night. It may not seem effective at first, but perceptible improvements can be detected gradually. The more time spent in body rubbing, the more firm the skin and muscles will become. Circulation, which is the basis of health, will be increased. As oxygen enters the body, toxins will be expelled. When circulation is flowing at its optimum, the skin will be nourished, the muscles will be toned and the nerve endings will be kept stimulated and alert.

What is meant by exercising the tendons? It means making a forceful stretching of all the tendons in the body so that these bands of connective tissue may be extended as desired. First, stretch the arms and legs and twist and turn the body until the joints are loose and able to bend easily. Then begin general calisthenics, including tumbling, to make the body even more limber. This training, if practiced daily, is highly effective for the development of body elasticity and agility. It is vital to make the tendons supple and flexible because these dense tissues unite muscles with other parts and are transmitters of the force exerted by the muscles.

Next, how can the student increase and deliver the inherent power of the different parts of his body? This is based on exercising with weights[1] to maximize the resistance power of the muscles, which, in turn, will increase striking power. The arms, legs, neck and torso can be strengthened with a precision regimen of weight training. Fist power is increased by continuous striking of punching bags. Jogging, running and jumping enhance leg power while advancing physical endurance. Eventually, when the body is considered to be in perfect shape, Ch'i training may begin. Ch'i literally means "air," that mixture of gases, chiefly nitrogen and oxygen, surrounding the earth. This vital element is the basis for human life. In the Kung Fu sense, Ch'i has come to mean an "inner strength." When Ch'i is combined with the word Kung, the result is defined as "the dynamic power of the air." Its essence is a focused mind-power which is propelled by determined willpower through the body. This directed mind-power energy is based on the absolute prerequisite for life—breath. As Chinese masters say, "He who knows the art of breathing has the strength, wisdom, and courage of ten tigers." Ch'i grows through the nourishment and cultivation of proper breathing. This growth is accomplished by disciplined sessions of meditation while performing variations of light and deep breathing.

Discipline is sometimes thought of as "training through suffering," but in this case we mean the exercise of profound reflection through slow and determined effort. This exercise will not hurt. There is, instead, the exertion of an intense concentration which nurtures the inherent Ch'i. An immense charge of vitality results as Ch'i pervades the body. This dynamic fountain of energy may be stored inside the body for future use at will. However, Ch'i cannot be acquired immediately. It takes time. Serious contemplation cannot be rushed. Beneficial results only occur after a naturally time-consuming process. Anyone who tries to force the growth of Ch'i by any other means than possession of a calm or serene spirit may be compared to the ignorant man of Sung, who, upset that his crops were sprouting so slowly,

[1] The ancient Chinese used stone barbells with a two- or three-inch-diameter bamboo stick.

attempted to help them by pulling up the stalks a little each day until he pulled out all the roots. Without roots nothing may be nourished or cultivated. So it is with Ch'i. Properly developed Ch'i always has solid roots. Correct training makes it possible to use Ch'i Kung whenever necessary.

Since respiration is a natural part of our lives, this means that everyone possesses Ch'i, although few know how to summon their "inner strength" and use it at will. However, it can be mustered, without training, under high stress circumstances. It seems that every nation has its version of the story about a frail woman whose son or husband was pinned beneath an overturned vehicle. Acting with a supremely determined desperation to save her loved one, she alone lifted the thousand-pound-plus weight, which freed the victim. Or the tale of the father whose family was trapped by a raging fire inside their home. The man, supported by overwhelming resolution, broke through the wall of flames and carried out his wife and baby, who suffered burns but he himself was not marked. Not even a hair was singed. These are examples of untrained powers of Ch'i. They deal with directed energy. Normally, a small woman could barely lift one hundred pounds, if that, and a man running through sheets of fire would suffer at least third-degree burns, if not worse. These stories indicate that there is a higher level of power at our inborn disposal.

As physical strength is summoned, Ch'i becomes highly abundant for selected direction. Chinese masters have said that, if Ch'i is concentrated in the abdomen, the abdomen will become strong as an iron plate; in the back, the back strong as a copper urn; in the head, the head strong as a stone ball. If power is concentrated in the legs, the body will be "as immovable as Tai Shan Mountain." If strength is focused in the arm, it will be as strong as a pillar; in the finger, the finger will be as hard as the tip of a sword. These are examples of directed strength which indicate that the total mind and physical power may be delivered by one movement through a single part of the body without obstruction against an aggressor. If students exercise patience along with prescribed training programs, and adhere to the "five restrictions" and "seven detriments," the mastery of Kung will be inevitable, as ancient sifus contended.

Shaolin monks felt that no matter which style of Kung Fu was practiced, the practitioner must concentrate his "spirit" and isolate himself from temptation so that "evil spirits may not enter or inner demons may not attack." Where there is no evil, there is no disruption. Purify the thoughts by listening to one's own breathing, just the sounds of inhaling and exhaling. This was Shaolin "internal purification," which was a prerequisite for Kung training. By harmonizing one's inner system, sickness will be prevented, and the "spirit" will be elevated. Purifying one's desires, regulating one's breathing and concentrating one's efforts are the beginnings of Kung practice. Allocate ample time to accomplish these basics, which will help provide dynamic results later. For instance, old masters claimed that, if an adept meditated deeply while gritting his teeth, periodically swallowing saliva, illnesses of the internal organs could be avoided.

Kung Practice and Age

The ancient Chinese believed that anyone who had Ch'i was powerful and therefore could practice Kung at any age. While this is true, it is actually easier for a child to progress in Kung training because of his basic innocence. A child has a more receptive and retentive mind and can be better directed to utilize his intrinsic Ch'i. An adult, on the other hand, might have his practice plagued by devious thoughts, the "Seven Outer Passions" and the "Six Inner Desires," as the Chinese called them. Our inner systems may be attracted and influenced easily by these temptations. However, a child, "possessing a body of the pure positive element," would not have to contend with such distractions. He could attain quickly the necessary purity of mind and tranquillity of spirit for successful Kung practice, but it might take an adult many years to rid himself of "evils and demons." This is why Chinese martial artists usually began training their sons and daughters almost from birth. They would exercise their infants' limbs and rub their skin and muscles to stimulate and strengthen their growing little bodies. The exercise and massage would provide definite health benefits—better muscle and skin tone, improved circulation, balanced metabolism and a general feeling of relaxation and vigor.

When a child could walk and balance himself, he was then taught the rudiments of fist and leg fighting. This infant training became known, commonly, as "Womb Kung." Thus, Kung Fu training, admittedly not limited by age, is still more rapidly and effectively mastered by youngsters who grow with the art and are able to study and develop advanced techniques and philosophical refinements when they reach adulthood.

If practitioners can master just one of the many forms of Kung, though they may not be immune to bullets, they will definitely strengthen their bodies and safeguard themselves against attack. While the means of practicing the various kinds of Kung are naturally different, there is one strict rule, usually unspoken, that is the same for all—Never seek to harm others. Should a wayward or errant expert waylay others, not only would he be violating the basic precepts of the art, but the misapplication of his privileged knowledge would lead inescapably to his own destruction, whether by death or imprisonment.

As an old maxim put it: "The man of violence never yet came to a good end." On the other hand, a man of peace should be cognizant of death-dealing procedures, to be able to defend against them and to prevent the taking of life whenever one is able to do so. With this life-preserving perspective in mind, we shall present some of the most common and some of the most uncommon types of Kung which have been practiced during the past millennium.

Since some Chinese had a penchant for elaborating on their prowess in the martial arts, we will not suggest that anyone should immediately begin practicing any or all of the following Kung forms without proper guidance. Our recommendation is that a prospective student should discuss those forms which interest him with a highly reputable sifu in his neighborhood.

Most of the training routines that we are offering as examples of Kung exercises must be considered as extremely time-consuming and not widely practiced today. However, from the historical standpoint in Old China, when time was not usually thought to be of great consequence, ten years' devotion to master a chosen defense technique was commonplace. In those remote times, Kung Fu adherents engaged in a strongly disciplined program of active dedication and long contemplative study of their arts. Whereas modern materialistic civilization has a tendency to avoid sustaining and continuous self-control and to ignore or depreciate contemplation. Some of the following Kung methods are certainly possible to accomplish, but others must be viewed as fantasies designed to astound. Although it must be said that the impossible goes only as far as man's determination.

In the following sixteen examples of Kung, some of which have never before been described in English, we have relied heavily on an ancient Shaolin text written by an obscure monk scribe, Wu Toy San Ling Qung, who revealed the dynamics of Kung Fu in the *Treasured Secret Book*.

Again, for personal health and safety, should anybody wish to start practicing one of the selected Kung techniques, practice some basic common sense first.

RED SAND PALM

Red Sand Palm is one of the most astounding of the Yin Kung, or negative, elements. Without touching an assailant's body, the adept merely makes signs of rubbing or striking at him with the palm of one's hand from a distance and the receiver will be injured. The wound will cause irreparable damage. Death usually follows in ten to fifteen days.

The first requirement to achieve this distance killing practice is a basin full of very small-grained sand. (The red sand found in China is extremely fine grained.) Using both hands, scoop up some of the sand. Close the palms over it. Then, in a grinding motion, attempt to pulverize the sand grains. Mentally decide that not a single grain will sift through the hands until it has been reduced to powder. For best results, the practice session should continue with more scoops of sand until one is exhausted. Perform this exercise daily until, after a few years, the rubbing motion of the empty palms, even a few inches from the basin, can move the sand in it. Then refill the basin with course-grained sand. Repeat the same procedure several more years until the sand moves when rubbing the empty hands a foot away from the basin. Next, use iron beads followed by iron balls weighing approximately five pounds. When one is able to rub sharply the palms two or three feet over the basin and cause just one iron ball to bounce out, the art will be accomplished. Should a Red Sand Palm expert be forced to use the palms to strike an attacker at a distance, depending on the sharpness of the rubbing or striking hand motion, monk Wu Toy wrote that the opponent would "either collapse dead on the spot or die within two weeks." However, it is believed that this Negative Kung is so rare that no one in modern history has mastered it, although there are a few who continue to try.

ONE FINGER KUNG

One Finger Kung is another astonishing example of negative (Yin) power. This single finger concentration exercise is similar in function to Red Sand Palm. Begin the practice by suspending a heavy iron bell, a hundred pounds or more, to chest level in the middle of a hallway of one's home. Poke the bell with the right forefinger to make way every time one passes it. Initially, the weighty cup-shaped vessel will not readily respond to finger strikes, but with determined practice the bell will begin to sway back and forth from what seems to be a mere touch. And after two to three years of focused training, the bell will give way by poking at it sharply from two feet away. At this stage one will also be able to ring the bell by concentrated poking at the bell's hammer from a yard away.

After the bell ringing is accomplished, the next training level calls for the placing of a lighted candle in a quiet room. Stand between ten and twenty feet away from the candle and point at the flame with the right forefinger. At first the candle only flickers normally, but after disciplined practice for several years, depending on one's mental effort, one's finger pointing will extinguish the flame. Then place a candle inside a paper lantern and practice by pointing at the flame until it wavers unsteadily and dies while the lantern remains undisturbed. Next, attempt it with a glass lamp. If one can mentally manage to put out the flame by pointing at it

without breaking the glass, he will have mastered the art. At this advanced level, should the forefinger be aimed at an opponent, even though separated by a door, he still could be injured or destroyed. The Chinese considered One Finger Kung, which they say never missed, to be superior to Red Sand Palm.

DRAGON CLAW KUNG

Dragon Claw Kung, also known as Chin Na Palm,[2] has the effect of making an attacker feel as if a sharp talon has torn into his flesh as a master's five fingers grab onto various pressure points of his body. During basic training, using the fingers of the stronger hand, attempt to lift a small-mouthed jar weighing approximately thirty pounds. Even though it is empty, one may find that the vessel slips easily out of his hooking grip. However, after several months of diligent digital application, and directing the strength of the forearm into the fingers, one will manage to raise and

[2] For modern Chin Na techniques, see Chapter 5.

lower the large jar as he wishes. One is now ready for the next step. Pour one bowl of water into the jar prior to each practice session. The adept will gradually build up his gripping power until he is able to lift the jar, brimful of water. In subsequent training, using the same procedure, replace the water with sand, a bowlful each session until full again; finally, exchange the sand for lead beebees. When one is able to pick up the jar filled with lead beebees, part of Dragon Claw Kung will be accomplished. The fingers will possess the positive (Yang) element.

In advanced training, put the jar aside and practice the same hooking finger grip empty-handed with dynamic tension. Do this every morning at sunrise by pointing the five developing fingers toward the sun and act as if you were trying to grasp the distant celestial body. This empty-handed gripping practice enhances the strength of the negative (Yin) element. The Yin and Yang must always be harmonized to achieve ultimate effectiveness. Dragon Claw Kung employs both at different stages. And when practicing the dynamic tension grip, the positive element is avoided and the negative element is produced. If you are able to relinquish the use of the positive element strength, you will have achieved the ultimate in

Dragon Claw Kung. At this pinnacle, "birds flying across the sky will fall as if shot by arrows at a stretch of the gripping fingers. Wild horses can be managed as if bridled and the reins in one's hands." If this "Dragon" hand is used to grab an antagonist's pressure point in his arm, the limb will be immobilized immediately or temporarily paralyzed, but his life will be spared. Dragon Claw Kung, obviously capable of inflicting serious injury, nevertheless is used only to detain or restrain an opponent.

WATER DIVIDING KUNG

Water Dividing Kung is cultivated by concentrating strength in the backs of the palms and arms. The student should begin by burying a dozen ten-foot-long bamboo poles vertically three feet in the ground. Securely braid a rope in and around the top part of the straight row of poles, creating, in effect, a bamboo wall. While tightly bound together, the two-inch-diameter bamboos will remain slightly flexible. Thus, they could be forced open by superior strength.

The disciple starts his practice by pushing both hands through the center of the bamboo row, then spreads his arms outwardly as if he wished to penetrate a mob of people to save a trampled child. As practice increases, a small gap will appear; eventually one will be able to bend open the bamboo poles and walk through to the other side. Then, add another pole at each end of the row. Practice until the poles can be forced open with ease. Repeat this training until twenty bamboos are planted. With the planting of one bamboo, the weight force is increased by seventy-five pounds, which means that one would ideally possess fifteen hundred pounds of dividing power in his palms and arms. Should an unruly crowd ever detain an adept or block his passage, his Water Dividing strength will have the force to part the mob as an earthquake splits the ground.

HING KUNG

Since most of us weigh well over a hundred pounds when fully grown, it seems highly improbable that we could ever attain the freedom of lightness enjoyed by butterflies perching on tree branches or swallows flitting through the willows. However, it can be facilitated through the gently nimble art of lightness, Hing Kung. This rarely practiced Kung begins easily enough by filling with water a one-hundred-pound earthen vessel, which becomes obviously quite heavy, at least solid enough to support a human body as a student balances himself on the rim of the big-bellied jar. The student then ties two pounds of lead weights onto his body and walks, carefully along the edge of the vessel. He continues this practice daily, for approximately a month, until he can agilely step around the rim without falling off or knocking over the filled vessel. Next, he empties a cup of water from the vessel while adding five ounces of lead weights to the body. This procedure is repeated until he becomes twice as heavy and yet is able to walk along the edge of the eventually empty vessel. The following step calls for replacing the earthen vessel with an empty reed basket. It is filled with rocks and the student walks along the basket's rim. Gradually the rocks are removed until he can step along the edge of the empty basket. When this level of accomplishment is achieved, the student will be ready to

practice light walking on sand. Using small-grained sand, he paves a foot-path of about one foot deep, three feet wide and ten feet long. The path-way is covered with rice paper, which is as fragile as the wings of a dragonfly. As one first walks on it the weight of the feet will cause the porous paper to rip against the soft sand underneath. One must mentally and physically practice this light walking until he can step over the path without tearing the paper. Then, the ultimate practice—the paper is re-moved and the student walks on the sand until no footprint appears. The art of Hing Kung is then mastered. Thus "neither does a grass blade move when walking on grass nor a footprint show when walking on snow." And when the disciple removes all the weights from his body, his future jour-neys will never leave a trail. As fabled as this sounds, even monk Wu Toy admits that it takes over ten years to master Hing Kung. Do not step into this practice lightly. It will take profoundly heavy thought and supremely applied devotion to make your body as weightless as a cloud.

SPEED RUNNING KUNG

Speed Running Kung, also known as Night Walking Skill, is another cat-egory of Hing Kung, or "Making the Body Light." Leg and lung develop-ment is primary in this Kung, with eyesight training mandatory at the ad-vanced level. The initial practice is prepared by attaching lead weights equal to three per cent of one's body weight onto each ankle. For exam-ple, a one-hundred-fifty-pound person should tie a four-and-a-half-pound weight onto each ankle. Then run daily in an open field until winded. Do not, however, go beyond the stamina limit: rather run a little farther each day to increase the personal endurance. Every two weeks add a half-pound weight to each ankle. Continue the progression until the weight on each ankle equals ten per cent of your body weight (fifteen pounds per ankle for a one-hundred-fifty-pound person). In the beginning your body will find this training intolerable for long-distance fast running. However, after several years you will be able to run ten miles a day with ease while wearing the heavier weights. You must then continue to maximize the vi-tality by racing up and down hillsides. Advance this durability training by running up and down rocky cliff or mountain sides. Intensify the power running until the strain of the weights is not felt as leg maneuverability be-gins to resemble a sure-footed feline. The student will thus be ready to remove all the weights from the body, which will feel as light as a hum-mingbird.

Eye training is next. This is a most serious practice which must be con-ducted in a dark and quiet room. Place a lighted lantern covered with thin light green paper in a corner. Sit calmly approximately ten feet away from the lantern. Stare straight at the lantern until just before the point of strain, then close and relax the eyes. Stare and rest again. Repeat this twelve times during the evening. It should be stressed that this vision exercise must be practiced extremely slowly and patiently over five years to avoid any se-vere, trying or wearing pressure on the eyes. At first the lantern's wick is turned up, creating a bright light. Gradually, turn down the wick until the flame is eventually extinguished. If one can still see the lantern in the dark-ness, the eye training will be accomplished. Armed with these cheetah-run-ning and lynx-eyed seeing abilities, you will truly be as a cat—a lithe ani-mal of superior vision and physical dexterity.

飛行功

一二

LEAPING KUNG

Leaping Kung must not be ignored, no matter which style of Kung Fu one practices. A student should have basic knowledge of this Kung, even if he does not emphasize its development. Obviously, making a standing broad jump of five feet is nothing special, but when one can leap over a car or jump across a fifteen-foot-wide mountain stream, then this becomes a spectacular skill. And it can be achieved. Begin by digging a hole in the ground two feet deep and three feet wide. Stand in the trench and leap to the ground level. Repeat this jumping move until you are fatigued. Weights are also used in Leaping Kung practice. Every fifteen days add two ounces of weights to the body and dig the trench one inch deeper. Keep up a steady and determined progression as the weight becomes heavier and the hole gets deeper. Continue this for three to five years until able to leap out of the same trench, now over seven feet deep, while wearing over ten pounds of weights. Imagine, removing the weights and given some running room, how far the disciple would be able to jump!

WALL CLIMBING KUNG

Can man emulate a gecko, a harmless small lizard, streaking across the side of a wall? Kung Fu experts say yes, labeling the training Wall Climbing Kung, or, more commonly, Gecko Crawling. They claim that anyone well versed in this art can, with his back against a wall, move freely on and along the surface, horizontally and vertically, by using the controlled strength of his heels and elbows. While perfection of this Kung is indeed similar to a gecko darting as a matter of routine up virtually any wall, it certainly is not easy for humans to master precarious Wall Climbing, which often threatens to create great insecurity or instability. Generously estimating, one out of a hundred students might consummate this Kung.

Should you seriously wish to practice (because that is the only way a student will ever accomplish it—with extremely serious dedication), begin by lying on your back. Brace the body weight with the strength of the heels and elbows. Arch the body upward and slowly crawl on the heels and elbows. Perform this exercise for one to three years until you can lie on your back and move with the dexterity of a four-legged, long-bodied reptile. Then construct a solid brick wall, ten feet tall and ten feet wide, with the bricks protruding unevenly from one to six inches. With your back against the wall, place your elbows and heels on the edges of the protruding bricks and move along gradually with the center of gravity aimed toward the wall. At first the disciple may fall off without even getting both feet off the ground, but he should not be discouraged. Continue this Climbing practice until you are fatigued, for two sessions a day. After several months you will begin to get the "feel" of Gecko Crawling and in a few years will be able to freely traverse vertically and horizontally along the rough wall.

Then tie a five-pound lead belt around your waist and practice. At your own pace, over the next few years, increase the weight of the belt to thirty pounds. If you still can advance with ease across the uneven wall, you will be ready for the next step. Gradually begin hammering off the protruding bricks. Continue the training with the weight belt until the brick wall is hammered completely smooth. This little by little brick-chipping process will take no less than five years, probably longer, for ultimate success. Finally, remove the weights from your body and glide along the wall gracefully and silently. The student will have become a gecko master capable of following any lizard's path across a wall. However, a total of ten years' assiduous training is required to reach this lofty level of Wall Climbing proficiency. So, with a decade of dedication at stake Gecko Crawling rarely is achieved, with most disciples falling by the wayside.

TSIEN YIN KUNG

Many men have agonized over the fact that their testicles were located in such an exposed position. Why should these sex organs hang loosely outside the body? Doctors tend to agree that normal body temperature is too hot for essential sperm production. They maintain that the scrotum, the pouch of skin that contains the testes, provides a cooler environment. During regular fetal development two egg-shaped "balls" lie within the abdomen, but just before or immediately after birth they descend into the scrotum, where they remain extremely susceptible to injury. Striking a man's testicles will cause instant excruciating pain. Should the blow be hard enough, he will be incapacitated to the point of being unable to do little

功陰歛

more than bend over in agony while cupping his crotch area with his hands. His anguishing, almost paralyzing inability to defend himself will last at least thirty seconds, usually longer, again depending upon the impact force against the genital glands, although certainly offering the assailant sufficient time to do what he wishes.

Tsien Yin Kung is designed to avoid this possibility by protecting these delicate and normally vulnerable organs. This is accomplished by focusing the Ch'i to draw up the testicles into their original body orifice, that is, whence they came as a babe. Thus, one's vitals will not be harmed by outward attack. Some categorize this inward concentration under Internal Kung, which is not correct. In the Internal method Ch'i fills the entire body, racing through the arteries and veins and the four limbs so that no catastrophe, such as fire or freezing cold, can destroy a master. One will not need such superior Kung to avoid a human conflict. Rather consider Tsien Yin Kung, a negative concentration element, as a Soft Kung technique of avoiding mayhem. When first training, meditate without interference and rid the mind of all devious thoughts and anxieties. Then focus the Ch'i into the genitals. Follow this by concentrating this energy upward toward the lower abdomen. Continue this meditative practice for at least one year. Do not be impatiently rash or the Ch'i will dissipate and the spirit will become exhausted. One will be inclined to give up Tsien Yin Kung as being impractical. However, this Kung is possible. With correct focusing upon the cremasteric muscle, which surrounds the spermatic cord, one can draw up the testicles inside the body. Some men are known to be able to do this naturally at will with no prior instruction. Should the student not be one of that unusually endowed minority, he will experience nothing in early training, but gradually with devoted practice whenever he concentrates his Ch'i into the genitals, his scrotum will expand like a small balloon slightly inflated. When the potent Ch'i is forced up, the testicles will be attracted until they follow the Ch'i into the safety of the body cavity. Only the fleshy scrotum remains outside. He may regard Tsien Yin Kung to be perfected when he can thrust his Ch'i into his testicles and raise them during a dangerous situation. The scrotum will contract and the testicles will be harbored from harm.

BAG KUNG

A disciple will not require a real bag to practice Bag Kung unless he wants to label his belly as a kind of "superbag." Bag Kung means the cultivation of Soft Kung of the abdomen to make it like Amida Buddha's bag, which was full of Ch'i (he was the itinerant fat Buddha who always carried a traveling bag). One's "bag" will be to develop, in particular, the abdominal muscles surrounding the stomach cavity to protect it against frontal attack. When first training, meditate daily by concentrating Ch'i into the abdomen. Using both hands, first to the left, then the right, smoothly but firmly stroke downward thirty-six times against the abdominal wall. Then release the Ch'i and sweep upward thirty-six times, again using both hands alternately. Practice this for approximately two years. The abdomen will become as soft as cotton, yet the concentration of Ch'i will make it as solid as steel. Next, bury two wooden posts two and a half feet from each other with a wooden brace connecting them near the top. The posts should rise no more than four feet, i.e., to the level of the abdomen. Loosely mount a six-foot-long log across the brace. Place your abdomen against one end of the log. Suck in the stomach so that, in effect, the end of the log is wrapped tightly by the abdomen. Then pull back the body. You will fall back easily

功袋布

二九

leaving the log, but as the training intensifies, the end of the log slowly will be engulfed by the abdomen as if it were rooted in the pit of your stomach. Even though you may jerk the body back violently, the log still will adhere to the abdomen. And after the log is drawn in by belly power, a concentrated release of outward Ch'i into the abdominal muscles will cause the log to shoot straight out for several yards. Armed with this advanced ability, should an antagonist try to hit a master in the stomach, he will not avoid his harmful effort; instead the adept will accept freely his hard-thrusting fist while absorbing it into his abdomen. Not only will he be unable to withdraw his fist, but it will be painfully seized as if tightly locked in handcuffs.

It can be released with a sharp burst of outward abdominal Ch'i, which will snap the opponent's hand back causing his body to reel around, if not fall down. However, Bag Kung is seldom practiced anymore, since it takes more than ten years to master. Although its Soft Kung principle can and should be pondered often: the passive is used to restrain the active and the soft is used to restrain the hard.

IRON FOREARM KUNG

Iron Forearm Kung, also known as the Iron Pole, is thought to be one of the simpler and easier-to-master Kung Fu techniques. This arm training begins by lightly striking the inner and outer forearms against a firm, upright wooden support, for example, a balcony post or house pillar. Practice this exercise for fifteen minutes a session, twice a day. Six months later begin hitting the column harder. You will notice that the forearms can accept and tolerate the steady striking. They gradually become strengthened and hardened. Continue this for six more months. Then advance the training by pounding the forearms against a heavy tree trunk covered with coarse bark. This will enable the skin, muscle and bone to develop more resistance against a rough and hard surface. Practice this for at least an hour a day for two years. Repeat the same procedure but use large rocks instead of a tree trunk. Strike smooth rocks at first, later uneven ones. Finally, concentrate on the rough rocks until a disciple can swing his arms freely and from any direction instantly shatter one with either arm. The arms, now with the strength and hardness of lead pipes, are potential lethal weapons for the preservation of peace. This, then, is Iron Forearm Kung.

功鞍馬

三九

FIST KUNG

Fist Kung has the effect of producing a steel battering ram out of the hand. One fist strike to the chest, for instance, can cause immediate death resulting from massive internal hemorrhage and shock. Usually only masters who dedicate their lives to the martial arts manage to perfect Fist Kung, while many others disregard this Hard Kung as being unnecessary for the attainment of the true essence of Kung Fu.

The simple reason is that you must first break the main knuckles in your hitting hand, normally the first two, sometimes four. This is done by smashing the fist against a rock. The joints at the roots of the fingers will break after repeated heavy blows, causing the rounded prominence of the struck knuckles to flatten. Allow the knuckles to heal. Then slowly begin hitting a light smooth rock and start building a layer of calluses over the previously broken knuckles. Continue this until a solid callus has formed over and between the knuckles and one is able to strike the rock while feeling no pain in the hand. Next, begin hitting a fifty-pound rock with the fist. At first it will be difficult to budge, but with constant practice the rock can be moved. Replace it with a one-hundred-pound mass of rock. Punch it until you can put the rock into motion. Now, use a boulder weighing about three hundred pounds. Strike it one thousand times a day. This sounds like a lot but this exercise can be accomplished in less than an hour.

After two years of this advanced training, if the student can project the boulder even two feet with one bash of his fist, he will have mastered Fist Kung. However, at this lethal level, his fist will have literally no other function than that of a pile driver. Equipped with this tremendous striking force he must be very careful that he does not hurt innocent people or break property unintentionally. Old masters thought of this and always used their lesser used hand, i.e., if they were right-handed, the left hand was developed for Fist Kung.

SANDBAG KUNG

Sandbag Kung is classified as a Hard Kung, although its mastery does not rely entirely on the strength of the Yang element. Training methods require the construction of a sturdy wooden frame as seen in the picture. Depending on one's reach and height, the square frame should measure approximately five feet a side and stand eight feet high. Suspend ten ten-pound sandbags equally around the four top beams. Using a strong rope, firmly secure the ten-pound bags so that they hang at the chest level. Step into the center of the framework and assume the Horse Stance or Bow Drawing Stance. Strike the sandbag directly in front of the right fist. When the bag swings back to its original position, hit it harder. Continue this practice until your accuracy and timing are enhanced with precision punching at the swinging target. Each stage should last three months, five days a week, five hundred strikes for each hand during the daily session.

In the second training stage, the disciple should strike two sandbags facing him with both fists at the same time. During the third stage, he uses the fists alternately in a left-right hitting procedure. When one sandbag has been struck to the peak of its outward arc, the other bag should be swinging back to its original position. Again, he is conditioning his timing and accuracy. After the student has perfected the forward thrust punching, he will be ready for stage four.

In the fourth stage, intensifying the peripheral vision by hitting the two bags at one's immediate left and right, the student strikes the bags with

功包沙

四
一

both fists simultaneously, hitting them again at the bottom point of their downswing. For the fifth stage, the same two bags are hit alternately. After becoming proficient in striking sideways, he practices the drill together with the striking forward exercise.

In the sixth stage, the two forward bags are punched with both fists at the same time, then immediately the side bags are hit with both fists at the same time. The student continues this hitting exercise as he times the punches at the lowest point of the downward arc of the returning four bags. When he is thoroughly precise with this training level, he continues to stage seven by alternately striking the same four bags, hitting one forward bag, then one side bag, continuing by punching the other forward and side bags. In this advanced drill, the reactions must be instantaneous. If one is slow or the timing is off, he might be struck by one or more of the returning sandbags. That means he will require more determined practice. When stage seven is mastered finally, he will be ready for the more complicated stage eight.

The student uses both elbows to strike two forward bags at the same time, following this by hitting two bags in back of him with reverse elbow blows. Then he alternates by striking one forward bag and one near bag. He continues by hitting the center bag facing him with his head. Also, he uses his head in striking the center sandbag behind him. Then, using both shoulders, he simultaneously strikes two bags in the front, followed by knocking two bags in back of him, alternating as in previous drills.

Next he combines the elbow, shoulder and head methods with the stage-seven techniques. With total effort he will be able to punch all ten sandbags consecutively without having a single one return to hit him or get by his follow-up blow while he remains in a stationary stance. The Sandbag Kung is nearly accomplished. Stage nine is the last training test. Gradually, the student harmonizes the stance with the body movements and moves his footing according to the striking actions in stage eight. If, in certain positions, he is using both fists to hit two sandbags, as more are rapidly returning, he strikes the others with the feet, knees, elbows, shoulders and head. At this level, should ten vicious street fighters gang up on the disciple, his reflexes will be so lightning fast that none of them will be able to penetrate his defense. At the same time, anyone being struck by one of his assorted blows would be as a hit sandbag sailing backward.

IRON BROOM KUNG

With the legs serving as "brooms," opposition may be swept away with the application of Iron Broom Kung. Leg strength development is the key to this Kung, especially emphasizing the concentration of power in the lower legs. Do not expect too much from the initial training. The student might even find it strenuously boring, but it is quite necessary to form a solid foundation for Iron Broom Kung. Begin by merely practicing a low Horse Stance each day for a specified time, although the word "merely" may offer false confidence, because remaining in a low Horse Stance for longer than fifteen minutes creates a painful strain on the leg muscles. Depending on one's physical attributes, start with five- or ten-minute sessions and work up to longer time periods. Do this gradually over a year's time to avoid overexertion or extreme soreness of the legs. During the second year of this rigid stance training, as one practices for longer periods he

will feel the heavy strain turn into a kind of numbness in his legs. If tolerance and durability are not developed correctly, once he moves a foot to stand straight, he may fall down from exhausted legs and suffer a brief inability to walk.

He practices (about two years) until able to stay in the low Horse Stance for one hour without the legs feeling overtired. With such a solid stance at his command he is ready for the next step. Bury a seven-foot post four feet into the ground. The post should have a three-inch diameter. Sweep kick it with either one leg or both legs, as you wish, for five hundred times a leg, each day, five days a week. At first, the post will not budge when being kicked, but little by little it will move until at last the kicks will break it. Replace it with a five-inch-diameter post and repeat the same procedure until this bigger one breaks. Next, replace the training post with a large tree that has a trunk at least a foot thick. One may think that attempting to kick the tree down might be compared to a dwarf trying to shake a mountain; however, following a year of circular sweep kicking the tree trunk, he will see improvements. The reverberations passing through the tree from the powerful kicks will cause the branches to shake slightly and some of the leaves to fall. Gradually the trunk itself will be shaken noticeably. Two years later the adept will find that one of his kicks against the trunk will cause the entire tree to shake to the point of cracking with a rain of leaves falling around him. At this level of leg power proficiency, should any number of assailants want to do him harm, none would be left standing through his use of Iron Broom Kung because his low spinning kicks would be as the autumn winds sweeping leaves across a meadow.

JADE BELT KUNG

Jade Belt Kung arms the body with the binding and crushing strength of a powerful bear hug. Training is considered simple although rigorous. Select a large tree and as you face it assume a low Horse Stance. Wrap your arms around the trunk and clasp your hands together. Squeeze tightly with a steady lifting effect as if you were trying to stand up straight, but do not release the firm grasp. Practice this pressure exertion exercise for a half an hour a day, five days a week. Squeeze the arms with full pressure for three minutes and relax for one minute. Repeat these two steps for the duration of the exercise. Initially, you will find that constant tensing is a definite strain for three minutes, but after two years of arm bracing practice, you should be able to squeeze powerfully and continuously the tree trunk for at least fifteen minutes. When hugging the tree a slight shaking motion from the arms will release a shower of leaves. At this level of achievement your concurrent lifting strength development should reach the point where even the roots of the tree may be pulled up. Next, for Jade Belt Kung to be fully effective, repeat the tree trunk girding procedure with a five-hundred-pound boulder. At first you will not be able to budge the huge, unwieldy rock. However, at the end of two years' practice of arm "belt tightening" you should be able to pick up the rounded and worn mass of rock and handily walk with it locked securely in your arms. This is the attainment of Jade Belt Kung. Supported by this massive clasping and grasping power, you will be able to destroy the natural condition of, say, a strangler who attacks a master in the dark of night. Your arms could crush the killer's ribs with the ease of breaking match sticks between your fingers.

功帶玉

四
九

It is told that there was a blind boy, filled with hate, who sought murderous reprisal for his father, who had been slain by a brutal brigand. The youngster's eyes had been slashed to prevent future identification. His blindness also prevented the boy from learning Kung Fu, or so he lamented. One day while he was tearfully bemoaning his youthful plight along a roadside, a Shaolin monk passed by and happened to hear his grief-stricken story. The thoughtful monk decided that Jade Belt Kung would be a suitable art for the sightless boy to practice. The enthusiastic youth perfected this Kung in four years of extraordinarily dedicated training. This brave but still blind Jade Belt Kung master then began his journey on the roads to find his father's murderer. However, his feeling of outrageous hatred had dissipated through the teachings of the monk. The wise old man had counseled him that to avenge was permissible in certain circumstances, but to seek revenge could never be condoned. There had always been a distinct difference between these two methods of exacting justice. To avenge, the monk said, is to inflict punishment, either in behalf of yourself or of others, for the sake of vindication or just retribution; to revenge is to inflict pain or death in resentful or malicious retaliation.

For example, Shaolin monks felt it their obligation to aid in avenging the injuries of the helpless. With this attitude in mind the young man eventually succeeded in bringing a deadly justice to the wanton killer who had caused such enormous suffering. So it is said that Jade Belt Kung was one of the secret powers of the Shaolin monks and was only taught to exceptionally needy and gifted disciples outside of the temple.

HEAD KUNG

In the arts of Kung Fu a "hard head" is considered a protective asset which can be developed through the practice of Head Kung. Since the usually vulnerable head is always a prime target in hand-to-hand combat, an antagonist, determined to "beat the guy's head in," would be mentally stunned himself after a Head Kung master purposely accepted the punches by blocking them with his forehead or permitting his opponent to break his hands on his head. The element of surprise executed by literally "using your head" as a fighting weapon is enough to discourage or subdue any attacker. This art is categorized, naturally, as a Hard Kung devised to strengthen the surrounding tissue, mainly in the forehead area. To ensure mastery, the student must flood the brain with the preservative of internal Ch'i. Training begins by tying a long, thin sash around the head. Wrap it around twenty times before securing it. Remembering the prerequisite, first concentrate Ch'i into the head, then drive the forehead (with tolerable force) against a stone wall. The twenty layers of padding will serve as a cushion to avoid injury to the untrained cranium. However, it cannot be emphasized too strongly that, should one be unable to focus the essential energy of Ch'i into the head, this highly advanced Kung should not be pursued. Brain damage could result. With that warning, strike the head against the wall one hundred times a day, five days a week, for one year. (Ancient adepts said that 250 times per day was the preferred regimen.) Then remove one layer of the safeguarding cloth wrapping. Gradually, increase the hitting force to suit individual abilities. Remove one layer of the sash protector following each three-month period of subsequent regulated training. Continue this practice until all layers of the cloth are removed. At

the zenith of this art the head will become as hard as the stone wall. Head Kung will be fully accomplished when a master is able to chip off pieces of stone from the wall with his head serving as a hammer. Demonstrating the art will be a simple matter of breaking bricks with the forehead. The student can visualize what would happen if a street hoodlum tried to rob him by holding a gun to his head. One sudden, unexpected head blow could definitely crack the robber's skull, resulting in his instant submission (unconscious or dead), permitting police to be calmly alerted.

CH'I KUNG

Through extensive translations of ancient Chinese texts for this book, it has been determined that the practice of the various Ch'i Kung arts was fairly common in China. But this was hundreds of years ago when Chinese masters would willingly spend a lifetime in order to accomplish one or more of the internal power techniques. In attempts to assess what modern Chinese masters have been doing with these arts the authors, with the co-operation of the Ministry of Physical Education of Taiwan, arranged for a private exhibition which featured many of the finest Taiwanese masters of Ch'i Kung forms. After noting that all of the old books relied on drawings to portray the masters performing their amazing powers, it was decided that photographs could better demonstrate the abilities of contemporary masters. On this basis, approximately fifty masters from all over Taiwan agreed to perform in an auditorium in Taipei. They permitted their pictures to be taken for this book in efforts to let the Western world know that there are still people in the modern world who are mastering traditional Ch'i Kung arts. For instance, co-author Chow, personally witnessing and participating in one demonstration, rolled up the sleeves of his shirt as a master had requested. The master held his palms about an inch away from Chow's forearms. Closing his eyes, the master made a concentrated effort and applied his "red hot palms." Chow felt the heat of the palms penetrating into his forearms. As the palms slid down gradually toward Chow's wrists, still about an inch away, Chow felt his blood being pressured downward "as if the blood were about to pour from my fingers, and yet this master never touched me." Another example featured a student who held up a washboard with the corrugated ribbing facing his stomach. The student raised his sweater to show clean, unblemished skin around his stomach. The master stood about four feet away in front of the washboard. Then, after meditating for some thirty seconds, the master lightly snapped his wrist toward the washboard. He never touched it. He never touched the student. A dramatic moment followed. The student put down the washboard. He took off his sweater to reveal skin with reddish lines across his stomach. The lines from the washboard? Strange, but seemingly true.

While Ch'i Kung is still being practiced today in many Chinese-speaking communities around the globe, it remains a rare endeavor for a select few. It is mainly confined to the master-father instructing his family along with, perhaps, some of his relatives and close friends. It is extremely difficult for an outsider to become a student. True Ch'i Kung training is not readily available in the average commercial self-defense school. Because of the intense devotion and time investment, these powers may not be acquired in a regular training hall after two or three years. It does not seem to work that way with Ch'i Kung. For one thing privacy is mandatory for the learning of any of these arts. It would be difficult to master one of the techniques while studying with ten or twenty other students. It is possible but more time-consuming. Concentration has a tendency to be diverted in a noisy atmosphere. As a result, grand scale study of Ch'i Kung is impractical. It is not that some Chinese would not like to mass-produce Ch'i Kung masters. It is not because they want to be antisocial or secretive. It is just that Ch'i Kung is best mastered in a peaceful and private setting. The concentration and serenity factors must be considered for efficient mastery. It may be compared to a composer who would find it difficult to compose while listening to other music. Or, a meditator might find it difficult to concentrate quickly in the middle of a lecture hall audience.

The following photographs, taken by co-author Chow, show some of the examples of what Chinese Ch'i Kung masters are doing in this modern age. The photos demonstrate their internal powers. They show not so much how a brick or board is broken, rather how the human body is able to withstand the blows of hard objects. What happens when a master's back is struck by a steel bar? His back is not harmed but the bar is bent. A master is able to drive nails through heavy wood with his forehead. Imagine striking his head with your fist. Which would be stronger? A master is able to poke steel rods against his throat and bend them with no harm to himself. Would an attacker be able to choke that master?

This 22-year-old woman performed an exhibition with her father. She began by breaking five unsupported bricks, one after the other. She merely held up the bricks in one hand and broke each one with a single stroke of her other hand.

The hard style of Kung Fu, such as stone breaking with the edge of the hand, has been seen in the West as adapted by Japanese and Korean Karate experts. The Chinese master (at right) demonstrated an advanced form of stone breaking. Instead of the more routine shattering of the rock with one blow, he chopped two times and held up three evenly sliced pieces.

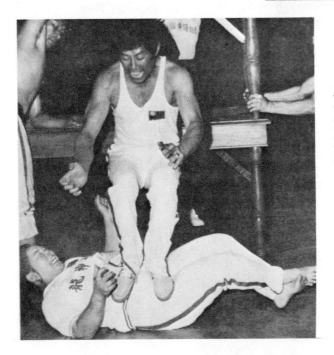

Jumping from a height of two tables and a bar stool, the husband gave a power inducing yell and landed on his wife's midsection. By concentrating her Ch'i she resisted the impact without harm.

Following her stirring demonstration the young woman poured the broken glass on a small mat. She took off her jacket and lay on the jagged glass while her father placed a four-inch concrete slab and six bricks on her stomach.

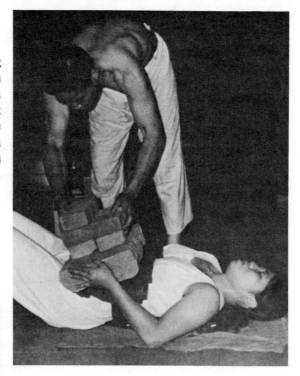

Her father took a sledge hammer and broke the concrete and bricks but only after three powerful strikes. By exerting her Ch'i simultaneously through her midsection and back she was able to accept the blows without injury.

This Chinese Ch'i Kung master concentrated his Ch'i into his vital temple area, the flattened side on either side of the forehead. He placed one side of his temple on the curvature of five files, the other side held four bricks, supported by an assistant. Another master took a sledge hammer and broke the bricks with one sharp blow. While the bricks shattered, the master got up and bowed to the audience. He was not hurt.

By concentrating Ch'i in the forehead this twenty-four-year-old Ch'i Kung devotee broke twelve tiles with one instant head blast.

A Kung Fu master's body must be extremely flexible. This suppleness and flexibility may be acquired through a program of prescribed stretching exercises, a requirement for any martial arts training. Astounding physical agility is possible as the Chinese master demonstrates above.

A team of young Ch'i Kung experts demonstrated some of their extraordinary accomplishments. A small bed of thirty nails, ascertained by some members of the audience to be sharp and hard, was placed against the stomach of an expert who assumed a horizontal position. One of his partners put seven bricks on top of the bed of nails, while another, using an outsize wooden hammer, broke all the bricks after several strong strikes. The young man on the receiving end of the force then got up slowly, still holding the nails against his stomach. He lowered the nail board, revealing an absolutely smooth stomach.

There were no marks, not even one indentation of a nail on his skin.

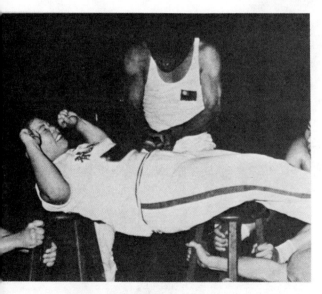

This husband and wife team demonstrated how Ch'i Kung can be applied as a shield around the abdomen. Not only did the wife avoid pain, but the quarter-inch solid steel blade was circulated through the audience. Six people stomped on it but could not straighten it.

This is an example of a hard form of Kung Fu rarely seen in the West. The master told the audience that he would break all of the bricks except the second one. After the Ch'i Kung elbow strike, co-author Chow examined the five bricks and, sure enough, number two was unbroken while the others split in two as specified. This high form of Ch'i Kung should be witnessed by Westerners to fully appreciate the controlled power of the mind.

After twelve strikes, the husband bent a one-inch-diameter steel rod to 45 degrees across his wife's back. Twelve people in the audience could not bend it back into place.

Ch'i Kung permits the body to be used as a protective shield. This master exercised his Ch'i through his back. The weapon was broken rather than his back which was unmarked. He felt the impact but without pain.

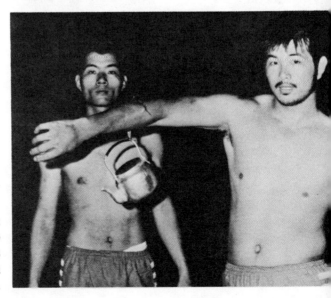

The young man's partner attached a tea pot on the piercing needle to indicate that the exhibition was performed in a definitely vital skin area.

Another young Ch'i Kung expert stoically accepted a needle through his right cheek. He did not display any pain or irritation.

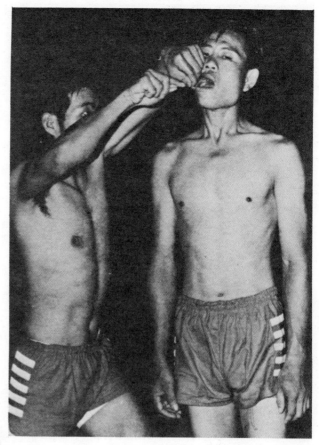

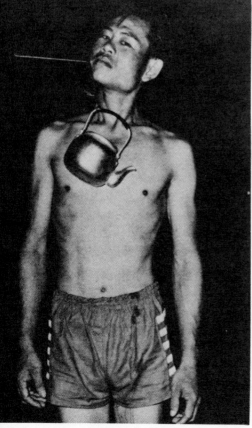

To demonstrate that the needle was firmly implanted into his cheek a team member hung a filled tea pot on the steel instrument. Note the drops of tea which had spilled on his chest and shorts. When both of the young Ch'i Kung masters removed the needles from their bodies there was no bleeding and there were no obviously discernible marks left by the "wounds."

A pliable body enables the master to choose between contention and non-contention. Acting on his philosophical belief of non-contention the master (above) shows an example of a concealment technique, in this case, inside a bamboo basket. Despite having the power to crush an antagonist this is certainly a most peaceful way of avoiding hostile circumstances. This is the ultimate victory of "no contention, no fight."

Using his bare forehead this 82-year-old Chinese Ch'i Kung master drove an eight-inch nail through four inches of board. His only precaution was the placing of a small piece of cloth over the nail.

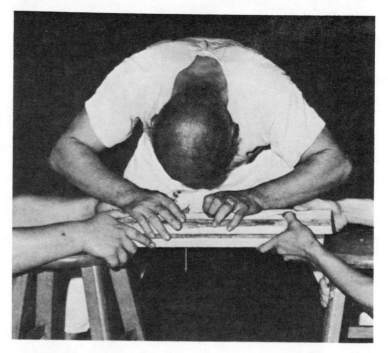

While author Chow examined the nail and felt the intense heat generated by the steel driven through the hard board the master (at left) displayed an unmarked forehead.

7.

Kung Fu
Hits Entertainment

It was in the year 1972 that Kung Fu made a rapid and sensational impact on the heart of the Western entertainment world. The main force behind the fast-emerging popularity of the Chinese martial arts came from the "Kung Fu" television series, which triggered a mass of Hong Kong-made Kung Fu movies hastily dubbed and adapted for the Western market.

Out of the midst of all the powerhouse entertainment came the matinee idol of all Kung Fu action films, the late Bruce Lee. Kung Fu movie smashes were feeling shock waves of applause and shouting approval from around the world. The dynamic oriental theatrics, seemingly so new and unusual, fascinated millions of Westerners who did not realize that elements of Kung Fu had entertained Chinese for thousands of years through acrobatic performances and the classic Peking opera.

This ancient Chinese entertainment incorporated elements of grand opera, ballet, comedy, tragedy, mime, the historical play, the circus and acrobatics. Only those most gifted in physical co-ordination and pantomime were accepted into a troupe. Many had prior combat training which was of immense aid in the portrayal of military men whose fighting prowess included some extraordinary acrobatics based largely on various forms of Kung Fu. Every actor had to master an enormously intricate series of body, leg and foot movements. Graceful action was the prime essential, coupled with precision. Flexed knees, high kicks and sweeping exit steps were all highly important. While there was no tradition of high dramatic art such as that which characterized Shakespearean England, the Peking opera, depicting scenes of comedy and tragedy from feudal life in ancient China, was the first art form to incorporate systematic styles of hand-to-hand combat techniques and weapons usage. These styles were choreographed with complete safety and pinpoint precision because of the tremendous talents of the performers. All members of the troupe, who took enormous pride in their physical prowess, performed their own stunts. Actors would burst out onstage at astonishing speeds, performing feats of tumbling, somersaults, jumping and kicking. Violent action was an integral part of most plots.

The heritage of the traditional Peking opera today continues only in Nationalist China and Hong Kong. Various troupes, such as the National Chinese Opera Theater from Taiwan, have traveled to the West in efforts to keep alive this rich entertainment form, but all English-speaking audiences have had difficulty in assessing its cultural value because it has always been presented in the context of the Chinese language. In addition, dissonant but traditional Chinese instruments, strange to Westerners, especially loud clappers, cymbals and gongs, tend to discourage non-Chinese spectators. However, the acrobatic artistry has never failed to astound a Western audience and for this basic reason we hope that this ancient entertainment will not fade away into history. But, if the People's Republic of China has its way, it will, and the sooner the better for the Chinese nation. The "New China," in its revolutionary fervor, has altered its theater and opera. The new government, fed up with the old theatrical themes of royal intrigue involving mandarins, courtiers and concubines, has purged the classics while replacing them with fresh dramatic, even melodramatic, stories of heroic escapades by workers and peasants against greedy citizens and aggressive imperialists or tales of oppression suffered at the hands of wicked landlords. The new plays were initiated by Mao Tse-tung's wife, Chiang Ch'ing, herself a former actress. They still include much of the symbolism of the traditional operas while embodying the realism of the Western theater. "Make the past serve the present and foreign things serve China" is a common Maoist slogan applied to the performing arts. The special acrobatic and combative skills have been taken from the shelved Peking opera and freely injected into the revolutionary dance-dramas. One of the favorites of the current crop of action-packed ballets is the *Red Detachment of Women,* in which a crotchety and despotic landlord, Nan Pa-tien, is chased, chastised and ruined by a bevy of stalwart ballerinas. Klaus Menhert, in *China Returns,* said that "the battles in the 'Red Detachment of Women' are all fought—notwithstanding the partisan rifles!—with swords and halberds, which are standard equipment on the traditional stage. There is also a particular kind of kick in the scenes of hand-to-hand fighting that I seem to remember from old times." Menhert recalls correctly in that the dramatic but effective head-high circular kicks have been acquired from the old opera techniques which were originally borrowed from Kung Fu styles in Northern China. Thus elements of Chinese martial arts continue to entertain the People's Republic of China.

Modern Chinese audiences are excited by sword fights or, more precisely, the choreographed sword dances based on Kung Fu maneuvers which enliven revolutionary theater. It must be emphasized that all "New China" entertainment is rooted in patriotism subtly or not so subtly compelling the audience toward the Maoist view of life—"Remember bitterness and think of sweetness." Motion pictures are vital in "serving the state" with yearly film attendance estimated in the neighborhood of a staggering four billion. But feature films have relied heavily on theater. We note that all of the ballet-opera stage productions have been made into motion pictures, and extremely popular ones at that. It has been reported that *Red Detachment of Women* has been viewed by at least six hundred million patrons.

Although actors' names are sometimes listed on theater programs, this is usually avoided because the Chinese prefer to give prominence to an entire artistic company rather than to one individual performer, no matter how brilliant the potential "star" might be. However, there is one Chinese national who became a great film personality. His story began some fifty-five years ago when this martial artist who wanted to become an actor left his native land to become the Chinese-speaking world's first and foremost fighting film "star." He is the legendary Kwan Tak Hing, who still has a devoted following of millions of Chinese cinemagoers around the globe after being typecast, for the past thirty-five years, as the illustrious nineteenth-century pugilistic hero of China, Wong Fei Hung. Off the screen, this extraordinarily dignified gentleman can be considered to be a kind of living "Wong Fei Hung." Kwan Tak Hing lives up to his theatrical appellation by being legitimately known as a highly respected master of the famed White Crane style of Kung Fu in Hong Kong. At the age of seventy-two, he remains strong, lean and healthy through a disciplined practice of meditation and proper breathing. This man of many parts also operates the

The most famous White Crane master in the world, Kwan Tak Hing, displaying a classic pecking stance in his film *History of the White Crane Heroes.*

Kwan Tak Hing Medicine Store in the Causeway Bay section of Hong
Kong. He offers traditional Chinese herbal treatments for most disorders
and, with his great anatomical knowledge, is called upon to set and mend
many broken bones and torn muscles. This is customary knowledge for a
Kung Fu master of his stature. Once, during a dinner with the authors in
Hong Kong, Master Kwan cured an aching case of bursitis of Dick
Spangler's left shoulder by concentrating his internal energy force and applying his hand for a moment to the sore area. A warm aura was felt as the
sharp soreness went away completely two days later and has not returned.

Now a veteran of eighty-four motion pictures, Master Kwan began his
theatrical career at the age of thirteen on the stage in China. When the
Kwangtung-born actor was only fifteen, but supported by intense Kung Fu
training, he landed his first acting role as a martial artist because the part
called for a fighting expert and he was the only one available. That "bit

Actor Kwan Tak Hing kicks an aggressor in a tearoom fight scene from a film based on a nineteenth-century pugilistic hero, *Wong Fei Hung's Burning of the Castle.*

part" sparked the emergence of the world's longest Kung Fu movie career. Master Kwan arrived in Hong Kong at the age of sixteen, subsequently appearing in his first film in 1935. He was signed for the Wong Fei Hung fighting action series and, with his constant youthful appearance, still remains active as an actor in Mandarin films.

Master Kwan says that he is quite pleased with the image he presents on the screen: "For those who know Kung Fu they will also learn something from martial art films. I always play the good guy; this means that the Kung Fu master is portrayed as a good man. Young people will want to emulate this kind of character; one who knows how to protect himself and others and yet is peaceful, courteous, respectful." Kwan Tak Hing has made a good impression on Chinese-speaking communities around the world for over thirty years. While most Occidentals have never heard of this long-reigning Chinese film king (Master Kwan does not speak English), should you ask any knowledgeable Chinese resident of any Chinatown, "Who is Kwan Tak Hing?" his face will light up with instant and admiring recognition. He is still the best-known Chinese actor living in the

Bruce Lee

world today. Even the late Bruce Lee, who was the most popular Kung Fu film star in the world, used to see and enjoy Master Kwan's movies when he was a youth in Hong Kong. Although the young revolutionary martial artist differed with Master Kwan's traditional stylistic approach to Kung Fu, Bruce still admired and respected the older artist's impressive achievements.

Hong Kong motion picture magnates Run Run Shaw and Runme Shaw, on the other hand, have been grinding out bloody action "Eastern Westerns" for many extremely profitable years. They have a basic winning formula: virtually no plot, weak dialogue, but an overwhelming amount of action. The oriental potboilers of lurid sensationalism could be made for well under $150,000 apiece with an almost absolute assurance of making a sizable profit. Of course, some of the martial arts action is quite impossible, which has offended Master Kwan's sense of artistic integrity. He says, "As actors, we all take some dramatic license but showing Kung Fu fighters jumping twenty-five or thirty feet in the air from a standing start is just incomprehensible. The audience never sees the trampolines which make this possible. . . . The Kung Fu feats that we show in our shows," Master Kwan guarantees, "are only those which can actually be performed in reality. Of course, I say that someone can still walk up an eight-foot wall with adequate training. What is impossible for many is possible for some."

The other electrifying Asian personality who turned on movie audiences in a brilliant career tragically cut short by death in 1973 was, of course, Bruce Lee. This amazing Chinese-American, who so dramatically yet authentically put the Chinese martial arts on the motion picture screen, was one of the strongest powers behind the popularization of Kung Fu in the West. As the son of highly entertaining Cantonese opera comedian Lee Hoi Chuen, Bruce got an early theatrical start by being literally carried into the acting profession in his first role as "The Baby" when he was only six months old. Inheriting his father's fast wit and flair for showmanship, Bruce became a popular child star with twenty Chinese films to his credit before he was eighteen. But, growing up in Hong Kong with its teeming millions pressed into close quarters, punctuated by sporadic outbursts of youthful street gang violence, Bruce was determined to get by on more than just his entertaining glibness. He had fists and feet and wouldn't hesitate to use them. He once admitted that he had been a real teen-age rebel, "a young punk who went looking for fights." Since he was such a volatile and temperamental child, his parents nicknamed him Chor Um Ding, Cantonese for "Never Sits Still." While refusing to back down before anyone, he soon realized that he did not have the necessary knowledge to support his usually unyielding stance. When he was thirteen he complained that he was being pushed around by some of his schoolmates, and persuaded his parents to let him take self-defense lessons. He tried practicing T'ai Chi Ch'uan with his father, but Bruce felt that its fighting advantages would be too long in coming since the slow-motion forms stressed internal well-being and was "more an exercise for the elderly." As an impatient teen-ager, Bruce wanted a more immediately useful Chinese boxing style. He picked Wing Chun, a direct punching system which can be mastered fairly quickly. With his enthusiasm bordering on fanaticism, he learned it rapidly from the best Wing Chun sifu in Hong Kong, the late Yip Man.

Armed with a new self-confidence at the age of eighteen, Bruce left Hong Kong for the United States to ensure his American citizenship. He hadn't been back since he was an infant. He traveled to Seattle, Washington, seeking employment and higher education. Recalling his defiant boyhood days when he was asked to leave most of Hong Kong's best schools because of bad deportment, Bruce decided it was time to "actualize" his potential. After getting a job at Ruby Chow's restaurant in Seattle, the ex-Hong Kong hellion who hated school disciplined himself to graduate from Edison Technical High School. With his hard-earned good grades he was accepted as a philosophy major at the University of Washington. When not working or studying, Bruce practiced the martial arts, never missing a chance to work out, even to the point of pounding a hard pad that he put up in the back of Mrs. Chow's Chinese kitchen. He would constantly smash it in between serving the customers. He gave some demonstrations at the university. He began to teach a select group. Among the special few was nineteen-year-old premed student Linda Emery, who found Bruce "both exhilarating and rewarding." Bruce felt the same way about the slim and attractive all-American-looking coed. They fell in love and were married at a small Seattle Protestant church.

At the same time, word of Bruce's outstanding Wing Chun abilities quickly got around the martial arts community of the Pacific Northwest. His reputation started to spread across the rest of the West Coast. He opened kwoons in Seattle and Oakland. Then, in 1964, it happened. During an impressive display of his one-inch punch at the International Karate Championships in Long Beach, California, Bruce was spotted by the right people. The Kung Fu master's film career was ignited after influential Hollywood spectators saw him knock a man head over heels with what seemed to be a mere flick of his wrist. That "discovery" led to his first break—the television role of Kato, the Green Hornet's sidekick. "The Green Hornet" series only lasted through the 1966–67 TV season, but that was enough for Bruce to make an everlasting impression despite wearing a black mask in most of his Kato fighting appearances. The mask, however, could not cover up his dazzling Kung Fu movements and showmanship. Then film stars such as Steve McQueen and James Coburn, seeking to enhance their talents with some Kung Fu training, asked Bruce to be their instructor. Bruce agreed, noting that many entertainers were asking him to teach them, "not so much about how to defend themselves or how to do somebody in; rather, they want to learn to express themselves through some movement, be it anger, be it determination or whatever. So what I'm saying is that they're paying me to show them, in combative form, the art of expressing the human body."

Meanwhile, Bruce was beginning to see new horizons in his own expression of Kung Fu as his life was undergoing such a tremendous transformation in the United States. While a master of the highly effective Wing Chun style of Kung Fu, he still felt limited because "ultimately martial art means expressing yourself honestly." He did not want to remain confined to any one "system." For example, he was restricted by Wing Chun's lack of high kicks. After voraciously reading most of the world's books on the martial arts, combined with his intense practice, privately and with other stylists, Bruce decided to express his own way of Kung Fu, on his own terms. He called his martial art "Jeet Kune Do." The Cantonese phrase figuratively meant simplicity, directness and unrestricted fluidity in expressing "one's original sense of freedom," as Bruce called it. Literally, "Jeet Kune Do" means "The Way of the Intercepting Fist," which became the title of a "Longstreet" television series episode written with his friend Stirling Silliphant, an award-winning film writer. Then after the fan mail started coming in, Bruce appeared in three subsequent "Longstreet" episodes and some guest shots on TV's "Ironsides," "Here Come the Brides," and "Blondie." But even with some rave notices he still lacked major screen credits and was simply unable to crack the casting system of big-time Hollywood. Besides that he was oriental and producers were not going to risk their capital on a relatively unknown Chinese Kung Fu personality. So a discouraged but still determined Bruce Lee returned to Hong Kong, where, on the strength of his modest success in America, Chinese movie producers were clamoring for his services. They were always on the lookout for a new star to beef up the already strong Chinese Kung Fu attractions. At first, Bruce was not convinced that Mandarin films were for him. He went out and saw a few dozen and pronounced them "awful!" He was particularly bothered by the fact that the actors were fighting all the time and exactly the same way. "Nobody's really like that," Bruce said. "When you get into a fight, everybody reacts differently, and it is possible to act and fight at the same time. Most Chinese films have been very superficial and one dimensional." He thought he could make some hard-hitting improvements. Inspired, Bruce signed a two-picture contract with Raymond Chow's Golden Harvest Productions that guaranteed him full authority to direct all fight scenes. While not making any fortune on the Chow deal, only $7,500 per film, Bruce was out to prove Hollywood wrong, that he was "going to be the biggest Chinese star in the world." His first Kung Fu film, shot in a village outside of Bangkok, was technically

Bruce Lee

"amateur-like," according to Bruce, employing two less-than-satisfactory Mandarin directors to eventually complete the picture. However, his incredibly magnetic presence on the screen was electrifying. His precision whirlwind of kicks and punches immediately established him, without any doubt, as the foremost Kung Fu film star in the world. Theater box office receipts proved it. *Fists of Fury,* made for less than $100,000, brought in nearly a million dollars in its first Hong Kong run. Adding to its huge success on the Mandarin circuit (Hong Kong, Taiwan, Singapore and Indonesia), *Fists of Fury* became a big hit in Sydney, Rome, Buenos Aires, Beirut and eventually on the North American Continent.

Pleased by the tremendous response to his first starring role, Bruce followed up with *The Chinese Connection,* his second Chow film, which was made on a back lot in Hong Kong. The plot was only slightly more plausible than that of *Fists of Fury.* Despite the simplistic crudity of the story Bruce singlehandedly scored another cinematic triumph. His powers of exciting and inspiring an audience simply could not be denied. "I have this intensity in me; it makes the audience believe in what I do," Bruce said, "because I *do* believe in what I do." The box office continued to support that belief, with *The Chinese Connection* outgrossing his previous all-time record breaker, *Fists of Fury.* Now, assured of stardom, Bruce renegotiated his deal with Chow on a fifty-fifty basis on all future projects. His third film. *The Way of the Dragon,* he said, was made strictly for the Mandarin circuit. Yet it was the first Hong Kong movie ever shot on location in Europe and the first to use an American Karate champion, Chuck Norris. Lee felt that the Kung Fu/Italian light comedy was not his best quality effort for a Western audience, but the Chinese theater crowds were larger than ever, elevating Bruce to oriental superstardom by breaking the attendance records of his first two Mandarin movies.

However, his "American dream" remained unfulfilled. He still wanted to become an American film superstar. He saw his chance in a Hong Kong co-production with Warner Bros. The Burbank-based film studio had already successfully distributed Run Run Shaw's production of *Five Fingers of Death,* the first of the Hong Kong-made Kung Fu movies to make a regular run at American theaters, that is, if one does not mention that U. S. Chinatowns have been showing them for over thirty years, in Chinese, of course.

Warner Bros. wanted to keep up with the lucrative oriental trend, the seeming successor to the Italian "spaghetti Westerns" and the Japanese samurai films. The studio picked up a script called *Enter the Dragon,* which would once and for all establish Bruce Lee as not only an American but international superstar. Bruce had been in only one other American feature film. That was the 1969 detective thriller *Marlowe,* starring James Garner. But, with Warner Bros., Bruce saw a new beginning; his improbable dream could be a reality. He would be in his first starring role in an American-made movie, and Hollywood talent, the best in the world, was coming to Hong Kong to make it an artistic and technical success. The superhero-ruthless villain story is a kind of Chinese version of *Dr. No,* out of the James Bond action series with a little *Terry and the Pirates* mixed in, although *Enter the Dragon* relies mostly on the human basics—fists and feet—and ignores guns and supersophisticated Bondian killer gadgets. Upon completion of *Enter the Dragon* Bruce's meteoric career couldn't have looked brighter. He was sizzling with success, but as he told his sensitive wife Linda, "I don't know how much longer I can keep this up." Prophetically, he couldn't. On the threshold of incredible stardom as the first Chinese-American with his name above the title in the biggest martial arts film ever made, Bruce died a month before it premiered in America. His sudden death on July 20, 1973, shocked his fans around the world, inciting monstrous rumors that he was poisoned, shot, even the victim of the mysterious "delayed death touch" at the hands of enemies. The Chinese press went so far as to include superstition as the cause of his death. Bruce lived in the Kowloon district of Hong Kong. Kowloon means "Nine Dragons." Bruce had always been known as "The Little Dragon." Chinese superstition has held that when a little dragon is placed among many big dragons, sooner or later the little dragon will be devoured. In reality, Bruce's death was not as mysterious as so many thought. "What Bruce died of," Robert Lee, his brother, said, "was edema of the brain, which was caused by an allergy to a certain medicine that he took." While in fantastic physical condition from constant exercise, martial arts training and special health foods, Bruce could not ward off a congenital defect that caused his death.

It seems that Bruce and Raymond Chow were working on a new script, *The Game of Death,* while at Bruce's Kowloon home. Actress Betty Ting-pei had a leading role in the film, so they drove over to her apartment to talk about some details before their dinner meeting with Australian actor George Lazenby, who was being considered for a major part. While at Betty's place the three were studying the script on that July twentieth afternoon with Bruce acting "quite normal," according to Chow. Later, however, Bruce complained of a headache. He apparently accepted a high-powered aspirin, Equagesic, offered by Betty. Equagesic is a prescription pain-killer which, in this case, had been given to Betty by her personal physician. In addition to that one tablet, Bruce imbibed only a few soft drinks that afternoon. About seven-thirty that evening Bruce complained that he felt ill. While Bruce said he would lie down for a little while, Chow went on to the restaurant to meet with Lazenby. Nine-thirty rolled around with no Bruce or Betty; Chow got worried and returned to Betty's apartment. As far as Chow could tell, Bruce was still asleep with no signs of the unexpected convulsions that he had strangely suffered once previously on May 10, 1973. But a horrified Chow was unable to wake Bruce. Betty called her doctor, Chu Pho-hwye, who came right over but was also unable to revive Bruce, who apparently was just moments from death. Dr. Chu then sent Bruce to the distant Queen Elizabeth Hospital rather than the Baptist Hospital just a few blocks away. Dr. Chu later testified, "I spent at least ten minutes trying to revive him. When he did not show any signs of improvement, it did not occur to me that the time was of great importance." Dr. R. R. Lycette of Queen Elizabeth Hospital reported that Bruce's brain was "swollen like a sponge," that the swelling could have happened in half a minute or half a day. Dr. Lycette maintained that it occurred "very rapidly" in Bruce's case. The leading authority to examine the cause of death was Dr. R. D. Teare, who was flown in from London to oversee the post-mortem. The noted professor of forensic medicine at the University of London concluded that Bruce died from an acute cerebral edema (brain swelling) touched off by a hypersensitivity to one of Equagesic's main compounds, aspirin or meprobamate or possibly by a combination of the two ingredients. However rare that might sound, Dr. Teare, a veteran of over ninety thousand autopsies, said that was the only feasible answer.

"He always told us," Robert Lee recalls, "he would rather die at a young age rather than have people look at him old and weak with a bent back and trying to go from one place to another just trudging along instead of being able to run and skip along as he would like." As a legend, he lives on, growing greater. His memory stimulates every student of self-defense. As an action showman, Bruce Lee will long be emulated but most likely never equaled. Bereaved at the loss of her inspirational husband, Linda Lee said, "He lives on in our memories and through his films. Please remember him for his genius, his art and the magic he brought to every one of us."

For a farewell tribute to his brother, singer-composer Robert Lee wrote and recorded a song that poetically sums up his life:

BALLAD OF BRUCE LEE

. . . On Nov. 27 in the year of the dragon . . .

At the dawning of the morning
on the hour of the dragon
High atop the hills of San Francisco
Life's greatest legend was born.

CHORUS

Into this world came little Dragon, Bruce Lee
His hands and feet fast, powerful and mighty.
It was easy for him to win world's acclaim
for he was strong and his will untamed.

In his search for reality
He found the tools of JKD
Many hours he would spend a day
trying to find some better ways.

Few people know what was left to me
His poems, arts and philosophy
And like a flash of lightning he's gone
But I know his memory will live on.
                    Sunrise Music 1975

While Bruce Lee revolutionized violent action films with his superior fighting skills, we are also quite concerned, from the standpoint of our deep personal involvement, with the peaceful path of "Kung Fu" entertainment.

The first beneficial force that released the floodgates of awareness into American homes was an ABC Television "Movie of the Week" called *Kung Fu,* which first aired on February 22, 1972. As the ABC-TV publicity release explained the theme of the movie—"'Kung Fu' . . . Kwai Chang Caine, a Chinese-American fugitive from a murder charge in Imperial China becomes a superhero to the coolies building the trancontinental railroad through his mastery of an ancient science-religion." That show, telling of a Shaolin priest seeking constant peace while capable of inflicting instant death, marked the real start of mass interest in the Chinese martial arts in the United States.

Heralded for its sensitivity, *Kung Fu* producer-director Jerry Thorpe felt that the timing was right to expand the Kung Fu trend into the American television market although he wanted to do it in an antiviolent way. Thorpe said that he saw "an opportunity to make a positive statement incorporating Chinese philosophy which is as basic and as beautiful as any philosophy ever written. Since I felt that we had lost much of our sense of morality during these times of violence in America, here was a chance to give an audience peace and brotherhood." However, Thorpe knew that it was impossible to spoon-feed "a message" to the fickle American TV audience. "I felt that the entertainment would come from the exotic aspects of the Kung Fu fighting sequences. For example, the concept of a hero who does not want to fight, tries to avoid it at all costs and is finally pushed over the brink, is an infallible formula in dramaturgy. I think people enjoyed tuning in, knowing that the stoical and soft-spoken Caine was going to take all he could until at last he had to express himself through his martial arts skills. This was compelling entertainment. But only rarely was anyone killed in 'Kung Fu.' Caine would simply dispatch an opponent; subdue him with no real sense of killing. We never showed any spurting blood. We never hit below the belt. And there were never more than three combinations of strikes in one action sequence."

Armed with a working script "very close to poetry," Thorpe had to find a star who had vocal artistry combined with natural physical abilities. Bruce Lee, who was in Hong Kong making action Kung Fu epics, was considered. But with huge profits already accruing from two smash hit feature films he had completed in Hong Kong, Lee was headed toward total financial security, not to mention superstardom, by making motion pictures in the Orient. After several transpacific telephone conversations with Warner Bros. executives, Lee decided not to pursue the starring role in the "Kung

Chow instructs Carradine in the fight-to-the-death scene in the original pilot movie of "Kung Fu."

Fu" television pilot film, since he felt he would have been locked in on one project for three or more years should the show ever make it as a successful series. Lee opted for the more appealing and lucrative major feature films which gave him more freedom and flexibility in his booming career. Eventually actor David Carradine was considered and selected.

Then there was the matter of authenticity. Would the Chinese philosophy ring true? Would the Kung Fu action scenes look real? Thorpe needed a technical adviser for the show. He talked to some stunt men. He talked to some quasi-martial artists. "Then someone mentioned David Chow," Thorpe recalled. "He had all the knowledge necessary for the martial arts scenes and obviously had the expertise regarding Oriental behavior." That is the way the first "Kung Fu" movie was made. It turned out to be a labor of love for everyone involved. In authenticating the script, research was conducted on ancient Shaolin Temple life and Kung Fu training. It was revealed that the original Shaolin Temple was burned to the ground in A.D. 617. It was rebuilt ten years later during the T'ang dynasty. It was enlarged again during the Sung, Yuan and Ming dynasties. The main temple

Training disciples of the Shaolin Temple in movements of T'ai Chi Ch'uan.

was called "The Temple of the Thousand Buddhas." Kung Fu training took place within this temple.

The Shaolin self-defense systems, as legend tells us, demanded the most severe all-round mental and physical training ever devised by man. Perfect physical conditioning was, naturally, a prerequisite, but intellectual pursuits were absolutely primary. Written and oral examinations were supposedly given to monks nearing the end of their training. They were tested on their precise knowledge of Buddhist history and philosophy and generally on what we may call Shaolin humanism i.e., the qualities of being humane, of having kind and gentle feelings, and of sympathetic concern for the welfare and dignity of mankind. A Shaolin master had to have the correct mental attitude when acting as a peace keeper in the midst of society's violence. Masters of the fighting art had to know how to exercise loving restraint. Should the Shaolin candidates pass the profound mental inspection, the physical hurdles remained. First, the individual monk was pitted against his fellow monks in actual combat. Since the training was designed to assist the monk to successfully meet the challenges of life, he had to be able to properly execute what he had learned from the monk masters. Therefore, the self-defense exam took place just as if he were to encounter a murderous brigand outside the gates of the temple. Examiners required full-force execution of techniques to ascertain if the would-be Shaolin master had truly perfected his art. However, the ultimate survival test was yet to come. The progressing monk was then asked to enter a long enclosed hallway leading to an exit gate of the temple. This hallway was filled with maiming or death-dealing devices designed to test his perceptions and reactions. He had to have the highest sense of perception combined with instantaneous reactions in order to survive the seemingly never-ending violence outside the temple. The monk entered the hallway to face an ingenious maze of armed dummies which were triggered by any weight or tension that the Shaolin contender exerted on the floor or even against the sides of the perilous passage. No two monks could ever undergo the same sequence of attacks because body placement inside the corridor determined exactly when and where danger would spring forth. It was said that there were 108 mechanical dummies all cocked to release various punches, kicks, knives, swords, arrows, etc., in potentially realistic situations. Depending on the monk's placement of body pressure as he inched his way down the corridor, it was possible to be attacked by several dummies at the same time. This was obviously a superior test to ensure the monk's future defensive abilities should he ever have to protect himself or others against numerous attackers. Of course, even the legends admit that many monks never made it to the exit gate, with a few killed and some carried back injured in what could be called the "superhuman test." Although there was actually nothing "superhuman" about the monk's hazardous trial; it was rather the final examination on his own enhanced natural abilities. How much enhanced was the always serious question. If the embattled monk successfully parried all attacks in his brief but torturous journey, he was faced by the final barrier—a huge bronze ritual urn blocking the exit. The heavy tripod vessel, embossed on either side with the powerfully elegant designs of a dragon and a tiger, was filled with red-hot coals. It had to be moved. Some ancient Chinese histories claimed that the urn weighed nearly five hundred pounds. No matter how much it actually weighed, the urn turned out to be a virtual branding iron, for the monk was supposed to use his forearms to lift the smoldering obstacle aside. As a result, his left forearm received a dragon brand, his right forearm a tiger brand. This Shaolin "fire brand" was an enduring certificate of mastery of Shaolin martial arts. It was a badge of respect and honor although it was usually concealed by the monk's long robes since he was not prone to publicize his hard-gained knowledge of Kung Fu. This part of the Shaolin legend, depicted in *Kung Fu,* was one of the most popular sequences of the TV show. In the television version Caine was shown fighting his way to the gate only to fall exhausted in the snow when he emerged from his ordeal. No one greeted him. Another Chinese tale asserts that master monks were always there to greet any new master as he opened the gate proving his worthiness not only to his Buddhist faith but to himself.

While modern scholars agree that there certainly was a Shaolin Temple, they tend to disagree about the accuracy of many of the Shaolin stories told and conceivably embellished over the centuries. How exactly true all the Shaolin stories are is extremely difficult if not impossible to ascertain. The one thing that we do know is that they have been and still are very entertaining. Shaolin tales continue to fascinate martial artists in particular and Kung Fu fans in general, whether they be Chinese or any other nationality. In our research, for example, we found that during the T'ang dynasty when the Shaolin Monastery became a favorite visiting place for royalty and literati, it also became the entertaining subject of poets. Famous T'ang poet Shun Ch'uan-ch'i described the scenery in *Visiting the Shaolin Monastery:*

> *Visiting this Buddhaland with a Song!*
> *Standing alone in a forest,*
> *The Pagoda of the Wild Goose[1] is weather beaten;*
> *The Dragon Pond is as deep and everlasting as time.*
> *The garden is refreshed by dew;*
> *The bright hall casts a shadow in Autumn.*
> *Returning on the path in twilight,*
> *Chanting cicadas are heard throughout the mountains.*

Chinese poets also used to write about the monks' enthusiasm for their martial arts training. It was written that monks would often miss their evening service of sutra chants while in the intense but enjoyable process of perfecting their swordsmanship. In *Miscellaneous Poems on Shaolin Monastery,* Ming poet Hsu Hsueh-mu related:

> *Ancient hall enshrouded with mist of incense,*
> *Swords and lances waved in the waning dust.*
> *It is not strange that the monks are fond*
> *of martial arts,*
> *For Tang Tsuan was once proclaimed General.[2]*

[1] The Wild Goose and Dragon Pond (below) were well-known Shaolin Monastery landmarks.
[2] Tang Tsuan was a monk master who once led a successful suppression of foreign bandits who tried to terrorize the countryside.

Chow (left) choreographs a fight scene with a blindfolded Carradine, who was responding only to sound.

Even during relaxed moments it was suggested that the monks were concerned with the mastery of their physical arts. Ming poet Chao Hung-tzu wrote in *Poems on Shaolin Monastery* that "In their leisure time, instead of steadfast spiritual pursuits, the monks discussed martial arts in the ancient halls."

On August 8, 1972, laudatory word-of-mouth "Kung Fu" recommendations had spread around the country. Following the second showing thousands of fan letters flooded David Chow's "Kung Fu" office. The nation loved it. The show had touched a national nerve, an extremely sensitive one at that—the thought of peacefully rejecting violence in a society filled with violence. Caine and "Kung Fu" came to symbolize peace and brotherhood, human qualities so often ignored in the mass entertainment media.

After further proving itself by gaining more viewers with each episode, "Kung Fu" won its place in the commercial TV ratings game. It was deemed a hit. It then became a weekly series in January 1973. And eventually the ultimate—"Kung Fu" became the number-one television program in the United States, displacing the CBS powerhouse "All in the

Family." In the week ending May 6, 1973, "Kung Fu" forged into the top spot as the highest-rated show in the seventy-market Nielsen ratings. One show reportedly attracted an attentive audience of some twenty-eight million people. That meant that the nation could enjoy a thought-provoking program which presented a radically different philosophy of life, a rare accomplishment in American television.

Just as Confucius said before his death, "The strong beam must break someday," the "Kung Fu" series has passed into network television history, but the aura of its goodness lingers on in reruns here and there around the nation and the world.

> *Man cannot for a thousand days on end enjoy the Good,*
> *Just as the flower cannot bloom a hundred days.*
>
> *Tseng-kuang*

Knowing that the integration of Eastern philosophy has worked so well with Western art forms, the entertainment field remains open for future mergers of such thought. For the true Chinese martial arts enthusiast, the best Kung Fu entertainment has to be the real thing—recognized Kung Fu masters putting on public exhibitions and demonstrations. This has been partially satisfied by a few modern Kung Fu attractions in the West. Masters from Taiwan and Hong Kong have already made considerable contributions to the Occidental awareness of Kung Fu in various public appearances, but it is hoped that further enlightening performances will be forthcoming from the birthplace of the Chinese martial arts, the People's Republic of China. One Wu Shu delegation has already toured selected cities of the United States in 1974.[3] The audiences witnessing the demonstrations were astounded by the masterful performances of the thirty-two men, women and children, ranging in age from ten to their mid-forties. Wu Shu was not their full-time profession back in the People's Republic, i.e., their livelihood did not depend on the performance of their chosen style of Kung Fu. Instead, Wu Shu was characterized as their lifelong avocation, a subordinate occupation or hobby pursued especially for enjoyment and accomplishment. Thus, the masters were all labeled "amateurs"—students, engineers, educators, etc.—who were demonstrating the new spirit of Wu Shu, which is designed to "cultivate the physical and mental health of the people." Indeed, the youthful performers demonstrated that youngsters are

[3] Remember that the People's Republic of China prefers the term "Wu Shu," while the West has become accustomed to saying "Kung Fu" when discussing Chinese martial arts. Basically, for our purposes, the two terms are interchangeable, despite the fact that "Kung Fu" does not mean "martial arts," rather a "well-executed accomplishment." "Wu Shu," semantically more accurate, means "martial arts."

Wu Shu exhibit, San Francisco, June 1974.

capable of strong personal discipline and precision co-ordination. Both on and off the stage, their courtesy was constant, their manners impeccable. While the adult performers radiated dignity and respect with their extraordinary personal polish, at the same time, any individual excellence was shared equally among the members.

As with the Revolutionary Opera troupe, there is no "star" system. Everyone in the delegation shared equally in the rewards or audience acclaim. The group performers were in such close co-ordination with each other that it appeared as if their demonstration involved one person with many shadows. The weaponry display stunned the crowds with the performers missing each other by hair lengths of their sharp swords and spears. The Wu Shu troupe leader, Kuo Lei, emphasized that the use of weapons was not to be considered warlike. Instead, the weapons were displayed as props and used as added weights for the performers to further synchronize mus-

Wu Shu exhibit, San Francisco, June 1974.

cle development for strength and grace. In effect, the Chinese performers showed that martial movements, usually thought of as deadly, can be transformed into the most graceful of physically spectacular ballet and menacing weapons converted into the most delicate of precision instruments.

They wanted Americans to realize that the New Chinese no longer think of Wu Shu as a system for aggression or even a militaristic art. Maintaining that Wu Shu has long been outmoded as a tool for warfare, the Chinese contended that modern military nuclear hardware has eliminated the mass need of hand-to-hand combat arts, especially those involving broadswords, spears, cudgels and halberds, which, we must admit, certainly are obsolete in this age. With the spectacular performances, acrobatic in nature and accompanied by taped music, the real message of the Wu Shu delegation was revealed. The performers, wearing the basic loose-fitting Chinese slacks and shirts, indicated that Wu Shu is practiced strictly for its physical benefits. Their main reason for dedicated Wu Shu training—through hard work and concentrated effort, it is possible to achieve seemingly impossible physical speed and agility while keeping the body in excellent condition.

Troupe leader Kuo Lei made it clear that a modern master in the People's Republic is never out to win at any cost. This attitude is in sharp contrast to the old feudal habit of killing or maiming an opponent. Wu Shu, the revised version, is a "sport to promote friendship." "Now it is sport with friendship rated first," Kuo Lei stressed, "and competition rated second."

Omitting all references to Buddhist or Taoist heritage, the People's Republic maintains that Wu Shu is "a cultural legacy which the Chinese working people have accumulated and enriched in their practice from generation to generation." Guided by Chairman Mao's great call to "promote physical culture and sports and build up the people's health," Wu Shu has, since the founding of New China in 1949, and particularly since the Great Proletarian Cultural Revolution, developed vigorously and spread through town and countryside like many other athletic pursuits. New China Wu Shu masters assert that the "sport" has been studied and edited based on the principles of "weeding through the old to bring forth the new" and "making the past serve the present," so that it can better improve the people's well-being.

Solo Kung Fu form or "set" competition and demonstrations have been popular at many martial arts tournaments, but all-out, no-holds-barred, face-to-face Kung Fu fighting has not been promoted in the ring, nor is it ever likely to be.

Understanding Kung Fu's true spirit of seeking the best in and for mankind while knowing the worst, that is as it should be. This means that if it takes rules or guidelines to make elements of Kung Fu into a "sport," then so be it. Following refinements of boxing and wrestling, even Judo and Karate, Kung Fu styles could be modified into "sport," that is, an athletic activity requiring skill or physical prowess. By omitting the lethal, nonsport ingredients of Kung Fu, it is hoped that properly regulated open tournament competition, with suitable safety factors, will be encouraged to sharpen the martial arts, to reach performance goals, and to realize the standards of others in free and friendly and, yes, even entertaining contest.

It appears that commercial enterprise is stretching its collective imagination to the limit in offering amusements and diversions, however ludicrous, to the modern Kung Fu enthusiast. The old monks would have been deeply saddened by the extremes to which their honored art has been taken. They would have been very distressed that their Kung Fu "way of life" was being drained of its philosophical essence, emptied of its "emotional content," and was being used strictly for physical "sport" development in their homeland. Perhaps those men of moderation would have been slightly more encouraged at the rise of martial arts demonstrations and tournaments. Kung Fu demonstrations, for example, have become a regular part of many Karate tournaments in the West. Some Kung Fu masters have even adopted Karate fighting rules in order to enter the tournaments. These attractions continue to help educate Westerners about the physical and the mental and philosophical values of the Chinese martial arts.

It seems that Kung Fu has just begun to entertain; that more and more Westerners will embrace the idea of not only seeing a martial arts attraction, but of becoming an active participant in Kung Fu.

True Kung Fu, as a total "way of life," can be highly entertaining. It can hold one's attention with proper performance.

8.
The Westernization of Kung Fu

The highest purpose of Kung Fu has always been to improve the condition of man by eliciting the advantages which he naturally possesses. The study of Kung Fu to gain those advantages is bound to increase, although a greater availability will have to be fostered for those who wish to learn Kung Fu in the proper spirit. Such opportunities are difficult to come by at this time in many parts of the United States. There are simply not enough recognized Chinese masters to go around. Unfortunately, most of the commercial Kung Fu schools now operating in America are but pale reflections of the original in old or even new China. But there are a few truly authentic, even legendary masters who live in the United States.

About thirty years ago Americans began to accept the importation of the better-publicized Japanese martial arts. For example, Judo, since 1950, has made some successful inroads at various colleges and universities around the nation.[1] In addition, Karate, Jujitsu and Aikido classes have sprung up at numerous campuses since 1960. During the last decade, a few Kung Fu classes or clubs have been organized on and off certain campuses, but, so far, not enough to make any significant or active impact on the youth of America.

[1] Despite considerable academic red tape and resistance to foreign sports, co-author David Chow started the first self-defense and Judo class at U.C.L.A. in 1951. It was sponsored by the University Recreation Association. David, the 1951 California State Judo Champion, started similar classes at U.S.C. in 1954.

The entertainment industry has been heavily responsible for kindling the smoldering fires of interest in Kung Fu. Most young people are acquainted with Kung Fu through the Bruce Lee movies and the "Kung Fu" television series—but that is about all. They might talk about it or even make silly jokes and assume a few fighting stances at times, but only a few of them understand enough of its real meaning to become actively involved as students of Kung Fu. This is why we would emphasize Kung Fu instruction at schools. The classes would stress nonaggressive techniques while providing excellent forms of: 1) physical exercise, more vigorous than regular physical education classes; 2) mental stimulation, learning something practical, useful and culturally beneficial; and 3) self-defense, which helps students gain confidence in their ability to take care of themselves. Obviously, students could not become experts through brief introductory or intermediate courses, but they could learn some of the basic self-defense moves and philosophy, which might, through competent instruction, stimulate them to study further without getting involved in perhaps unassured long-term commercial martial arts contracts off campus. They would gain the necessary knowledge, at least, to be able to distinguish a legitimate master from a fraudulent or unskilled "sifu."

Confucius summed it up by saying, "The cautious seldom err." In modern terms that means that the best defense against an aggressor, armed or not, is an alert and aware citizen. Therefore, with more Americans looking for more physical protection and "domestic tranquillity," general knowledge of the Chinese martial arts would help diminish violence in the streets. Since crime thrives on opportunity, "easy marks," such as the elderly, sick, crippled or intoxicated, criminals are much more apt to avoid someone who is walking tall, proud, aware of what is happening around him and self-confident in his knowledge of Kung Fu—as such he will probably be left alone or be able to offer help to those whom he sees in distress. Brutal violence against individuals can certainly be reduced if young people were properly trained in self-defense during their formative years. Masters can direct and apply the enormous youthful energy of the students to constructive mental and physical martial arts training, which would benefit them for the rest of their lives. Not only would students learn to avoid crime or fighting, the intense training itself tends to keep youngsters off the streets and away from meaningless pursuits. Because of its incorrect image as a "killer art" Kung Fu may sound attractive to rebellious youth. They may think it will provide the answer to their weakness. It will, but to their surprise and if they stick with it, they will become confident men of peace rather than frustrated men of violence. Even pent-up frustration may be safely and effectively vented through heavy Kung Fu workouts. The exercises, sparring and forms present a most suitable method of releasing overcharged emotions. Kung Fu, at the very least, can offer hope for any young man or woman seeking purpose in life, a constructive future in life.

With much of their psychological pain stemming directly from a distinct lack of order in their lives, Kung Fu has the potential of alleviating this discomfort by offering a firm yet acceptable discipline. Many of these young people, middle- and upper-class youths included, have never had to face a strong, disciplined approach to life. Lamentably, a systematized instruction was never provided, properly with love, in their homes. In addition, an adjunct of discipline is form. The concept of form, notoriously missing in so much of the haphazardness of modern life, is an integral part of Kung Fu. In lieu of "doing your own thing" with no intended purpose or design, beneficial psychological and physical changes will result if the person has some regulative or prescriptive form to apply to his actions. Through the concept of form, a patterned conduct regulated by custom and etiquette, young people are able to develop more mature outlooks and more understanding about the unity of themselves with the natural order. Not only does Kung Fu offer a mentally satisfying way of life with an orderly arrangement, but among its many systems there is a specialty to fit almost any human physical need. This is a big part of Kung Fu's future in the West because there is room in Kung Fu training not merely for the physically superior but for those who are handicapped or allegedly handicapped.

As a blind student of Kung Fu once put it, "I don't feel handicapped. I simply feel less advantaged without sight, although my other senses are, perhaps, much more acute than those of 'normal' people. Therefore, I think I have some advantages that 'normal' people will never enjoy. For instance, in my 'sticky hands' training I'm beginning to be able to sense what my opponent is going to do just a fraction of a second before he does it. This might sound impossible to you, but I can actually 'see' some of the opponent's maneuvers. Not all, of course, because I have a long way to go before I master deep concentration and meditation. But the training has already taught me that despite my lack of physical sight I can appreciate and delight in life as much as any man." In addition, legless, armless, even partially crippled but strongly determined individuals have studied Kung Fu. It has taught them how to deal with life. They definitely learn how to defend themselves, but more importantly, in securing their future, they learn a profound way of living and dealing with life's misfortunes. In the words of the *I Ching:* "The unassuming youth seeking instruction with humility gains good fortune."

United States law enforcement officials have used elements of oriental defense training for their cadets and veteran officers since World War II. Presently, most police academies around the nation teach a variety of detaining, control and self-defense tactics. At the Los Angeles Police Academy, for instance, Sergeant Gerald Mowat, the officer in charge of the physical fitness and self-defense unit, says that recruits are taught "a combination of martial arts—judo, karate, aikido, plus collegiate wrestling and basic rough and tumble fighting." With an all too brief but vigorous one hundred twenty hours of martial arts training in the five months of police academy instruction, Sergeant Mowat says, "This is not enough time to make a martial master out of any new policeman." Therefore, he says, "We must keep the instruction extremely simple with an emphasis on pain compliance holds since only five per cent of police encounters are defensive in nature. The recruits rarely master more than a dozen holds in the initial five month training period." Since policemen are mainly interested in the easiest and shortest disarming or detaining maneuver against a suspected criminal, they tend to dismiss the use of flashy or long fighting forms, such as a flying jump kick. In seeking the simplest yet most effective methods of making an arrest without injury to a suspect or policeman, some police training programs are beginning to recognize the values of the Chinese martial arts. Although Sergeant Mowat says that "the LAPD is not really actively or constantly looking for more techniques," he does admit that he would "definitely like to see more humaneness in police martial arts. And if you can show me some new holds that a small officer, male or female, can use with assurance against a much larger resisting suspect, then I would be the biggest booster for those techniques." Chin Na, which has been essentially untried in the United States, should be given a test in police training. This particular Kung Fu system could turn out to be a further aid in the safe apprehension of violent suspects. The techniques are rapid, efficient and truly humane in approach, since Chin Na restraining holds only inflict pain when the suspects resist. Suspects, in effect, subdue themselves through the "guidance" of the peace officer. Despite its capability, Chin Na training does not stress the destruction of an opponent, rather just enough application to pacify him. With its easy-to-learn and easy-to-remember joint locks, Chin Na is an ideal tool for better law enforcement. Its techniques are used by police officers in the People's Republic of China, Taiwan and Hong Kong. The only remaining problem in the United States is the lack of qualified Chin Na masters to instruct the country's crime fighters.

Barring major revelations from Mainland China the best places for Westerners to learn Chinese martial arts continue to be Taiwan and Hong Kong. For example, Master Chan Hon Chung, the chairman of the Hong

Kong Martial Arts Association, indicates that he wants the arts of Kung Fu passed on to the masses of people around the world. His challenge is to have open defense systems so that other stylists may study each other's techniques. In ancient times, with limited weapons, "your knowledge of fighting arts kept you alive, you were your own best weapon." Therefore, masters were very reluctant to instruct others in those days because of fear of eventual betrayal or that a disciple might become as powerful as he was, or, indeed, stronger. Many secrets have already gone to the grave with the masters who refused to reveal their last superior techniques. In efforts to keep the remaining knowledge alive, Master Chung related that currently there is a new attitude of sharing in Hong Kong. Masters are beginning to exchange knowledge of each other's style, but it is gradual. As Master Chung says, "After centuries of traditional secrecy, we cannot expect to achieve complete openness overnight." But through openness, he envisions a "brotherhood of the martial arts" which would assist in the elimination of neighborhood, cross-town or even international rivalries.

He also is an advocate of teaching Kung Fu to all students without regard to race, color or creed. This is in direct variance with the old Chinese martial arts thought that insisted that only Chinese, and selected Chinese at that, were to be instructed. One of the major hopes Master Chung has for Kung Fu is that it may spur peaceful bonds between different peoples.

Noting that the Chinese Martial Arts Association, made up of forty-five leading Kung Fu masters in Hong Kong, is only eight years old, Master Chung says that he has high hopes that his mission will be concluded successfully within five years. The sixty-eight-year-old master of the White Crane and Hung Gar Ch'uan systems has already come a long way by unifying the many diverse Kung Fu schools into one governing group. This was no easy accomplishment, with Hong Kong previously the scene of many a back alley or rooftop fight between rival martial arts schools claiming superiority of style. Gangster alliances, known as "Triads," also were known to study Chinese fighting techniques to strengthen illegal intentions. Hong Kong, a crowded seaport city which has banned the carrying and even the ownership of firearms, is still plagued by the criminal activities of the Triad societies. Triad members enforce their nefarious demands with strong-arm methods supported by the use of knives. The outlaws, executing basic Kung Fu techniques, obviously have helped to give the Chinese martial arts a black eye. However, it was the constant bickering between some of the recognized schools that led to corrective action. Respected masters were forced to protect the good name of the practice of Kung Fu after incessant challenges and insults were hurled at certain rival instructors and their students. This kind of thoughtless martial arts strife led to killings, serious injuries and the destruction of training hall facilities. Eventually, the responsible masters, envisioning the demise of authentic Kung Fu training in Hong Kong, decided to intervene and plead with the offending instructors to resolve their differences. Reason finally prevailed. They banded together to help rather than hinder their martial arts. In the furtherance of that goal and to avoid the influx of fraudulent "masters," Chairman Chung said that the association is planning to award certificates of recognition in the next few years. Only those possessing these documents should be recognized as legitimate. They will not be easy to obtain. First, of course, the individual must be a supreme master of at least one of the systems he practices. He must know and reflect the philosophical teachings of Kung Fu. Then, for the ultimate test for a prospective master, he must be able to communicate, to illustrate and to explain the moves and philosophy to students. Looking even further to the future, Master Chung said his main emphasis is "the opening of Kung Fu styles for international development to reap enormous physical and mental benefits." The Hong Kong Chinese Martial Arts Association has established a cordial relationship with Japan and is exchanging knowledge with martial arts organizations in Tokyo along with other Asian countries. Representatives of the association are beginning to make themselves known in Hawaii, California and New York.

But the Westernization of Kung Fu continues to be a slow process. For one reason, swift mastery is inconceivable. Kung Fu cannot be swallowed like a vitamin pill, resulting in a sudden surge of power. Overnight methods of learning do not exist, which quite possibly may leave many instant-result Westerners by the wayside. "See flowers on horseback" is an old Chinese expression that means it is difficult to appreciate something in a hurry. If absorbed too quickly Kung Fu will never have a chance to sink in meaningfully, with the impatient student remaining ignorant of its natural elegance and deep emotional content. Certainly there are those who will never be mentally or physically attuned to the rigors and pleasures of the esteemed Chinese teachings. This means that the future of Kung Fu in America will depend on the personal initiative of the prospective student. It will also depend on the quality of instruction available. While phony or incompetent Kung Fu instructors have become commonplace, true masters of genuine ability and integrity are still difficult to find in the West. For anyone, especially parents thinking of enrolling their youngsters in Chinese martial arts classes, it is advisable to avoid the "Karate" dojo (training hall), which has only recently become a "Kung Fu" kwoon. Despite the fact that Karate evolved from Kung Fu, the two martial arts are distinctly different. Commercial incentives have inspired many of the suddenly new but often unreliable "Kung Fu" establishments in the community. This means that the potential student should also disregard the school and absolutely any advertisements that guarantee results within a specified time limit. Since we all have different mental and physical characteristics and capabilities, precise developmental guarantees are ludicrous and promoted only by the fast buck artist, not the reputable martial artist. We all advance at our own pace. And, long-term written contracts, three to five years, are definitely not necessary for the student. Again, they only benefit the money-making purposes of the school. Should the student wish to change schools, become sick or injured, he would still be legally bound to make monthly payments—even from a hospital bed. The best advice is to personally visit a group session, observe and talk with not only the master but with the older students. If the advanced students are strong and graceful and act like respectful gentlemen and gentle women (women are becoming more and more attracted to Kung Fu) instead of wild ruffians, and if the master is who he says he is and positively proves it, the would-be student should join on a trial basis. A rapport must be established between the master and student. If it does not develop, leave the school because the master has the power to direct and influence the student's entire life. He should not be misguided. However, if good vibrations are there, almost akin to a loving father and child relationship, and if the style suits personal needs and disciplined progress is realized, then the student should continue his development at his chosen school.

In addition, much of the contemporary Kung Fu literature has been self-serving and of dubious quality, and, as we readily admit, books, magazines, and picture pamphlets cannot teach all the necessary martial art skills. Neither can films of forms and sparring, although motion pictures can offer another helpful dimension of instruction. The printed word, pictures and films may provide beneficial supplementary information, but only direct, face-to-face, personal guidance from a master will ensure effective physical and, indeed, mental performance in Kung Fu training. Students may then practice what they have learned on their own, alone, preferably in front of a mirror to heighten proficiency toward the ideal form. Practice at least three times a week, in two-hour sessions, to maintain steady progress. On the other hand, some of the more enthusiastic students are known to work out from six to eight hours almost every day. That kind of dedication is hard to find in these fast-moving times, but it is beneficial, when possible, because only through diligent training will a pure self-reliance ever be achieved. As Chinese wisdom tells us, "Those who endure most are rewarded most with perseverance making all things easy." And, during the training regimen the student must not forget that absolute mastery may be attained only through a framework of mental and physical togetherness and spontaneity. Philosophical precepts must be learned simultaneously with the physical forms. As ancient monk Master Han Shi explained this duality to his disciples, "The Shaolin way of fighting stresses virtue, but not force; defense, but not attack. The heart is affected as virtue spreads; the antagonist's will is suppressed as your Ch'i is summoned. Defense gives the chance to live; attack gives the chance to die. When others attack and I defend, my heart is at rest; my Ch'i concentrated, and my spirit lifted. All is in tranquillity. Thus, when Ch'i is abounding, no harm can come to me. Anyone who attacks me has lost his temper; his spirit is disturbed. Therefore, with his spirit distressed, his Ch'i scatters, and his strength, although great, dissipates in all directions with no defined focus of power. If you can handle a situation calmly in the midst of turmoil, you do not need to fight. The enemy will defeat himself."

Kung Fu is just like fire. If it is used beneficially, it will help one survive. If it is abused, it will destroy the user. As old Chinese masters said, "Misusing fire leads to destruction; misusing Kung Fu leads to self-destruction." Any martial artist must first cultivate his Ch'i. When this vital energy is in abundance, the spirit is perfect; when the spirit is perfect, strength is sufficient; and when the body feels relaxed, self-confidence is maintained. At this level, according to Chinese martial arts tradition before the establishment of the People's Republic, "no temptation can deter; no might can humiliate; no wind, rain, coldness or heat can harm; and no evils can disturb. If this level can be attained, one can practice Kung Fu without impediment." Chinese masters said that Ch'i is acquired through the understanding of life and death; apprehension of truth and falsity; purification of the mind; avoidance of worry; renunciation of desires; abandonment of selfish pursuits; and restraint of anger. While Shaolin masters told their monks that they should consider strengthening the body as the initial purpose of learning Kung Fu, the modern student should also comprehend the sympathetic quality of its Buddhist foundation which marked the true way of life for the monks. Too often the twentieth-century Kung Fu student will learn fighting techniques while avoiding the mental meaning behind the art. It must be understood, in the context of the traditional Chinese codes of behavior, that the art is to be used only for defense. "Do not assault for selfish reasons for fear that you might favor fighting which would end in your own downfall," Master Han Shi once said. "Constrain yourself to avoid burning yourself."

The major Eastern faiths have already attracted a small but growing group of adherents in the United States. For example, in attempts to blend with Western life, the Taoist Sanctuary in North Hollywood, California, teaches what Rector Khigh Alx Dhiegh calls "Neo-Taoism." Dr. Dhiegh says this is a concept of life "devoted to flowing with life within the context of *where* you are. Neo-Taoism is not so much concerned with how the ancients understood Taoism, but rather, how we may use the philosophy to help us understand and cope with the world of scientific technology in which we are living." With meditation, Kung Fu and T'ai Chi Ch'uan included in the teachings, Dr. Dhiegh says, "We're not trying to convert anyone to anything here at the Taoist Sanctuary; we are trying to convert someone to himself, to the discovery of himself. We make no judgments on good or evil because each must determine for himself what is morally good and bad whether the decision coincides with current societal precepts or not." Thus, the Taoist philosophy of natural independence is beginning to touch America, with many young people especially eager to learn of "The Way." Caught between the aggressive behemoths of big business and big government and possessed by his material things, the average American may find that Taoist or Buddhist tenets hold some possibilities for a more worry-free, even serene future. Kung Fu is an active distillation of those beliefs. In our sedentary-prone, urbanized civilization, Kung Fu contains the ingredients to foster increased strength and control of mind and body for the maintenance of a healthy society. Through a calm and intuitive understanding, the Kung Fu master builds solid character. The true master uses his strong personal foundation to perform constructive deeds for society.

At the same time, he deplores oppression and injustice. Several years ago some thirty people passively watched a woman murdered in the streets of New York without offering assistance of any kind, not even screaming for help. While a Kung Fu master certainly respects passive resistance, there is a limit to noninvolvement, even for him. He would have considered it his obligation to do his utmost to protect against criminal action he encountered or witnessed, regardless of his relationship to the intended victim. Whether it be an absolute stranger or his mother, he is bound to use his art to protect what is right. He will not stand aside passively during a murderous conflict because pacifism will not immediately stop an enraged or determined killer; it will not immediately stop a madman who suddenly wants to destroy everyone around him. Saddened, the master will act to stop vicious aggression and bloodthirsty destruction. He considers it necessary to exert his abilities in the midst of imminent and unavoidable danger of death or grievous bodily harm either to himself or others. As Lao Tzu might express it, "One may be compelled to redirect another's actions, but only as a *regrettable necessity.*" That regret, in modern Western terms, is the key to the legitimization of the use of force. The force or "redirection" is never executed with premeditated malice. It is always delivered with the proper amount of subduing power. There is no need to annihilate an aggressor. The only thing the master wants to annihilate is suffering, which, as indicated by Buddha's eightfold path, can be accomplished through right views, right decision, right speech, right action, right living, right struggling, right thoughts, and right meditation. Therefore, the master will attempt to disable the murderous assailant without killing him, although sometimes the attacker will die by impinging himself against the master's defense, in effect, killing himself.

The master, however, prefers to let the law decide the attacker's fate. As Buddha said, "He who deserves punishment must be punished. Whosoever suffers punishment does not through the ill-will of the judge but on account of his own evil-doing." Buddha continued, "His own acts have brought upon him the injury that the executor of the law inflicts. A murderer, when put to death, should consider that this is the fruit of his own act." Furthermore, the Kung Fu master will never intentionally violate nature's way by brazenly demonstrating his skill with persistent violence at the expense of others. That is the mark of a brute, not a man. "The good general never glories in what he has done," Lao Tzu said. "He fulfills his purpose, but only as a measure which could not be avoided." His intent is not to show off his superiority because superiority is the hardest kind of aggression to forgive. The reason—superiority is the most difficult form of aggression to return in kind. By revealing his mastery a Kung Fu master presents challenge enough, but to flaunt his superior fighting ability will eventually bring about his demise. True strength lies in noncontention. Sun Tzu, the brilliant strategist, said it best: "To win a hundred victories is not the zenith of skill. To subdue the enemy without fighting is the zenith of skill." However, there are charlatans who demonstrate empty fighting forms in feats of pretentious boasting only to withdraw in fear when confronted with an actual dangerous situation.

Fear has become such a distressing part of life in the United States that quite possibly this painful emotion may hold the key to the future direction of American Kung Fu. If fear can be eradicated, or lessened at all, through Kung Fu training, emphasizing its philosophical essence, then the Chinese martial arts will have performed a remarkable service. Imaginary fears might be purged first, the kind which can be compared to "the Kiangsu buffaloes panting when they see the moon, mistaking it for the sun." This sort of dismay or alarm is the easiest to get rid of, while the more intense kinds of fear—dread, fright, panic, terror, horror—are more difficult to eliminate permanently. These fears are so severe that a person so afflicted cannot move or talk. The strongly disciplined mind can keep fear at bay while using the natural emotion as a powerful stimulant. Thus, fear, properly understood, can serve as a valuable tool. "Fear is an instructor of great sagacity," Ralph Waldo Emerson said, ". . . that obscene bird is not there for nothing. He indicates great wrongs which must be revised." One revision that Western civilization might consider is its fear of death. It is important that we do not fear the darkness of death because fear itself is the only real darkness. To keep that darkness in the mind is to defeat ourselves. Expel it. Then it is not we who will be conquered, it is fear. Running away with fear still inside never gains harmonious freedom. Cowards never win noble victories. We must eliminate blind fear and ignorance if we ever expect troubles to be solved. "With Kung Fu," Chinese masters say privately, "you fear no man, you feel inferior to no man, you feel you can meet any challenge in life." They each feel as "secure as a huge rock," which is the Chinese expression for absolute security. They have come to terms with life and have no need of bragging about their "superiority." They, instead, seek an equality with others.

In this atmosphere, we hope that Kung Fu will continue to aid the dedicated American martial artist, and others, young and old, both sexes, in mind and body development through the learning of the modern styles of the classic Chinese self-defense arts. At the same time, the philosophical foundation will provide the necessary knowledge to attain ultimate proficiency in the art while successfully meeting life's constant demands. Since we do not believe that Kung Fu is just a passing fad in the United States, with the full force of the Chinese arts yet to be felt in the West, it is our assumption that opportunities will continue to grow with the strengthening of relations with the People's Republic of China. Of course, the determined individual who sincerely wishes to acquire the skill and philosophy of Kung Fu will certainly find the way.

Since it is impossible to escape the results of our deeds, let us practice good works. Let us guard our thoughts that we do no evil, for as we sow so shall we reap. There are ways from light into darkness and from darkness into light. There are ways, also, from the gloom into deeper darkness, and from the dawn into brighter light. The wise use the light they have to receive more light, and advance in the knowledge of truth.

Gautama Buddha

9.

Philosophical Vignettes

THE THORNY ROSE

Why should a peaceful nation have military forces and arms?

Why should a polite police officer carry a pistol?

Why should a friendly neighbor study the martial arts?
    And even more . . .

Why should a priest learn Kung Fu?

THE THORN DEFENDS THE ROSE AND HARMS ONLY THOSE
WHO WOULD STEAL THE BLOSSOM.

PAIN CAN HELP

If a man wishes to experience the joys and depths of life, he must not isolate himself on an island, emotional or otherwise. Nevertheless, if he associates with people and has relationships with people, he eventually will encounter someone who causes him pain. But he should not retaliate. He should not feel hate or seek revenge. Instead, he should feel grateful for the experience because without bad people and bad relationships how can he appreciate fully the good ones in the future?

KNIFE SHARPENS ON STONE;
MAN SHARPENS ON MAN.

A LONG PERILOUS ROAD TESTS THE HORSE;
A LONG PERILOUS JOURNEY TESTS THE MAN.

SEEK IN OTHERS

There is no perfect country.
There is no perfect society.
There is no perfect human being.

And every day there are so many kinds of people near you. People above you, people below you. People with whom you associate whether you work for them or they work for you. Should you wonder about the worthiness of these people, you must learn to accept them for what they are. But always look for quality in your fellow man no matter what his station in life. From this effort you can receive the most positive education that life has to offer. To understand humanity is to understand yourself and the world. However, when you recognize a person's imperfections and then condemn his faults, you too are at fault. Should you criticize someone, especially behind his back, you actually criticize yourself. That person does not hear the criticism. It does not do him any good. It does not do you any good. It is negative. Your words are wasted. Your time is wasted.

SELF-CULTIVATION HAS NO OTHER METHOD:
EXTRACT ITS ESSENCE FROM YOUR FELLOW MAN.

CONFUCIUS SAID THAT IF YOU RESPECT OTHERS
THEY WILL ALWAYS RESPECT YOU
AND IF YOU HAVE SYMPATHY FOR OTHERS
THEY WILL ALWAYS HAVE SYMPATHY FOR YOU.

TEN MILLION LIVING THINGS
HAVE AS MANY DIFFERENT WORLDS.
DO NOT SEE YOURSELF AS THE CENTER OF THE UNIVERSE,
WIDE, GOOD AND BEAUTIFUL.
RATHER, SEEK THE WISDOM,
GOODNESS AND BEAUTY IN OTHERS
THAT YOU MAY HONOR THEM EVERYWHERE.

THE PAST NOURISHES THE FUTURE

There was a man from a prosperous family. He had excellent health and was well educated but had an overwhelming compulsion for gambling. For a while he was lucky. He won a fortune by the time he was thirty-five years old. It was enough money to enjoy securely the rest of his life. But he decided to bet a little more in high hopes of winning a lot more. The gambler's luck failed. He lost everything. He was desolate. Instead of controlling his mental resources and approaching the following day as if it were the first day of his life, he felt sorry for himself: "I have nothing left." He pitied himself for weeks until the time that passed turned into months. Finally, after rejecting many jobs, the man managed to borrow some money from his family on the assumption he would start a profitable business. However, he later said to himself, "I'm going to win it all back!" He began to gamble again.

IF A MAN DWELLS ON THE PAST, HE ROBS THE PRESENT,
BUT IF A MAN IGNORES THE PAST
HE MAY ROB THE FUTURE.
THE SEEDS OF OUR DESTINY ARE NOURISHED
BY THE EXPERIENCES OF OUR PAST.

EQUAL BUT DIFFERENT

There was a group of children from the same neighborhood. They were the same age. They played the same games. They had the same teachers and graduated from the same school. These youngsters liked and disliked the same things. They grew into young adults. Although they were equal, each one of them became different in his special way. Different height, weight, strength and physical fitness. Different professions. Different financial incomes. Different emotional security. Differences in the amount of love and affection given at home. Some matured faster than others. And although we should accept the ways of others no matter what their levels in life, we must first respect our own way.

AS WITH LOTUSES IN A POND,
SOME LOTUSES HAVE RISEN TO THE WATER'S LEVEL,
OTHERS STILL REMAIN BENEATH THE SURFACE.
IN THE SAME WAY WITH LIFE
THERE ARE MEN DEVELOPING AT DIFFERENT LEVELS.

LIFE IS LIKE A BOOK,
NOT TO BE JUDGED BY THE COVER,
BUT TO TREAT EACH PAGE AS A DAY
IN THE LIFE OF ONE PERSON
AND TO REACH PAST THE COVER TO THE INSIDE
WHERE THE KNOWLEDGE AND INSIGHT CAN BE FOUND.
AND AS EVERY BOOK HAS A LAST PAGE
WE ALL HAVE A LAST DAY,
SO SHOULD WE THEN CONSIDER A BOOK
BY ITS CONTENTS
AND NOT BY THE NUMBER OF ITS PAGES.

WHEN MAKING THE FINAL ASSESSMENT
OF THAT ONE PERSON
WE SHOULD MEASURE THE DEPTH OF HIS LIFE
RATHER THAN THE LENGTH.

Bob Full, photographer.

Cary Chow,
translation, research,
and drawings.

Robert James Doran,
translation and
Hong Kong liaison.

Daniel Lee,
T'ai Chi consultant.

Ming Chen, from Shanghai,
contributed photos of
Wu Shu company from the
People's Republic of China.

Richard Spangler, co-author.

David Chow, co-author.

Daniel Shapiro, Mr. Chow's student photographed as attacker.

Curtis Wong, publisher of *Inside Kung Fu* magazine.

Howard Kaminsky, Mr. Chow's student photographed as attacker.

Index

98-99 Same Side Unnatural Grip Nikyo
100-101 Cross Hand Gokyo Otoshi
112-113 Men Tsuki, Jodan Block / Trim Atemi
114-115 Men Tsuki Gokyo + Take-Down
116-117 Kick TakeDown
118-119 Hammer lock escape
120-125 Kubi Shime escapes
126-131 Bear Hug escapes
132-135 Knife Attack Defenses